P9-CFJ-913

HE∧∨EN
RULES

HE∧∨EN
RULES

Take courage.

Take comfort.

Our God is in control.

Nancy DeMoss Wolgemuth

MOODY PUBLISHERS
CHICAGO

This book is based on the Revive Our Hearts series "Heaven Rules: Seeing God's Sovereignty in the Book of Daniel" taught by Nancy DeMoss Wolgemuth.

Some content in the foreword was adapted from Dr. David Jeremiah, *Agents of Babylon* (Carol Stream, IL: Tyndale, 2015).

All Scripture quotations, unless otherwise indicated, are from the Christian Standard Bible®, Copyright © 2017 by Holman Bible Publishers. Used by permission. Christian Standard Bible® and CSB® are federally registered trademarks of Holman Bible Publishers.

Scripture quotations marked NASB are taken from the (NASB®) New American Standard Bible®, Copyright © 1960, 1971, 1977, 1995, 2020 by The Lockman Foundation. Used by permission. All rights reserved. www.lockman.org

Scripture quotations marked ESV are taken from the *ESV® Bible (The Holy Bible, English Standard Version®)*, Copyright © 2001 by Crossway, a publishing ministry of Good News Publishers. Used by permission. All rights reserved.

Scripture quotations marked NKJV are taken from the New King James Version. Copyright © 1982 by Thomas Nelson, Inc. Used by permission. All rights reserved.

Scripture quotation marked KJV is taken from the King James Version of the Bible.

All emphasis in Scripture citations has been added by the author.

Names and details of some stories have been changed to protect the privacy of individuals.

Published in association with the literary agency of Wolgemuth & Associates.

Edited by Anne Christian Buchanan
Interior design: Erik M. Peterson
Cover design: Faceout Studio
Author photo: Katie Bollinger
Photo (on dedication page): Maria Peterson, used by permission.

All websites listed herein are accurate at the time of publication but may change in the future or cease to exist. The listing of website references and resources does not imply publisher endorsement of the site's entire contents. Groups and organizations are listed for informational purposes, and listing does not imply publisher endorsement of their activities.

ISBN: 978-0-8024-2952-0

Originally delivered by fleets of horse-drawn wagons, the affordable paperbacks from D. L. Moody's publishing house resourced the church and served everyday people. Now, after more than 125 years of publishing and ministry, Moody Publishers' mission remains the same—even if our delivery systems have changed a bit. For more information on other books (and resources) created from a biblical perspective, go to www.moodypublishers.com or write to:

Moody Publishers
820 N. LaSalle Boulevard
Chicago, IL 60610

3 5 7 9 10 8 6 4 2

Printed in the United States of America

Samuel Ethan Bollinger
June 13, 2021 – June 13, 2021

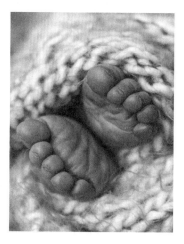

You never drew a breath on earth.

But with tears streaming down
and hands lifted up,
in a way we will never forget,
your heartbroken parents magnificently affirmed that

Heaven rules.

The LORD sits enthroned over the flood;
the LORD sits enthroned, King forever.
—PSALM 29:10

His dominion is an everlasting dominion
that will not pass away,
and his kingdom is one
that will not be destroyed.
—DANIEL 7:14

And there were loud voices in heaven saying,
The kingdom of the world has become the kingdom
of our Lord and of his Christ,
and he will reign forever and ever.
—REVELATION 11:15

Contents

Foreword

SHE'S PRINTED IT on her coffee mugs. It's the screensaver on her phone. It's engraved on a gold necklace hanging around her neck. It's featured in artwork hanging on the wall of her study, and she's produced it in a series of podcasts. Ultimately the message found in all these places became the full-length book you're holding in your hands.

Heaven Rules. It's short! It's catchy! And once you discover what it means, you will realize that it's life-changing. This message was birthed during the troubling days of COVID-19 when, according to Nancy DeMoss Wolgemuth, whose husband was also battling two unrelated cancers, "every day felt as though the sky was falling."

In case you haven't noticed, we are still living in sky-falling days. As this book is going to press, our American borders are overwhelmed with an influx of drugs and desperate immigrants. Inflation is out of control, with gasoline prices headed toward the stratosphere. School boards are erupting into riots as they fight over who has the right to educate our children. Many American workers are refusing to work, which means that companies trying to get on their feet after the pandemic shutdown are struggling to find employees. Escalating crime and poverty have reduced parts of the United States to developing-country status. Russia is at war with Ukraine, and little by little we can feel our nation being pulled into the conflict.

The details will be different in days and years to come. But the question remains: What do we do as Christians when we find ourselves in such frightening circumstances? We have only two options. We must make a choice between two *HRs*. If you walk down the hall at the headquarters of our media ministry, you will pass an office that is our HR office. It's our "Human Resources" department. HR = "Human Resources." And let's be honest, this is where most of us go when the sky is falling. We try to figure it all out ourselves. We trust our own resources and then we ask other *humans* to help us.

Nancy DeMoss Wolgemuth has a better HR plan to suggest. Her HR stands for "Heaven rules." And according to Nancy, "You'll never watch the news quite the same way again once you start to get a sense of what's going on behind those headlines, what God is doing on earth to accomplish His eternal, heavenly purposes" . . . when Heaven is ruling! Here in one short paragraph is how "Heaven rules" works:

> Though earth's happenings often seem random,
> meaningless, hopeless, and even cruel, what is happening
> in the heavenly realm is infused with such wisdom and
> goodness, with such a plan and a purpose, that if we
> knew what God was doing we would worship Him and

praise Him for whatever is happening around us, no
matter how it looks from our human, earthly perspective.

The phrase "Heaven rules" originates in the book of Daniel chapter 4, and it was spoken by Daniel himself as he tried to explain to a pagan king named Nebuchadnezzar what God was up to when He forced this king to roam the fields and eat grass like a beast for seven years.

To illustrate her "Heaven rules" thesis, Nancy takes us on a journey through the Old Testament book of Daniel and points out "Heaven rules" moments along the way.

Daniel lived the majority of his life in Babylon, history's symbol of the world's worst evils. Extreme decadence, infinite cruelty, ravenous power, and implacable contention against God describe this nation. But Daniel rose above it all. His autobiography reads like a modern-day rags-to-riches story. From his lowly position as a captive, he was promoted again and again, ultimately rising to the highest echelons in the government of his captors. Nebuchadnezzar made him ruler over the province of Babylon and chief administrator over all the empire's leading men (Dan. 2:48).

After Nebuchadnezzar's death, Daniel continued to serve the king's successors until finally, after Cyrus of Persia conquered Babylon and installed Darius as king, Daniel was made chief executive over the entire empire (Dan. 6:3, 28). In today's terms, he was the Persian Empire's prime minister.

Years ago I wrote a commentary on the book of Daniel called

The Handwriting on the Wall. When I signed that book for friends, I always inscribed the following verse next to my name: Daniel 1:21 ("Thus Daniel continued until the first year of King Cyrus" [NKJV]).

Sometimes a reader would return and ask me why I selected such a strange verse. And this was my answer. Daniel never stopped . . . never looked back . . . he just continued! He lived to see Cyrus, the Persian leader, conquer Babylon (October of 539 BC), some sixty-six years after Daniel had been taken captive. By this point, Daniel was over eighty years old and had lived a godly life in the public eye for almost seventy of those years. He'd outlasted some of the most powerful kings the world had ever seen. Daniel was able to continue because he knew the God of heaven and he knew his God was in control.

For all of the miraculous works God performed through and for Daniel, it's important to note that God never delivered Daniel from Babylon. Daniel lived his entire life as an exile in a foreign land—as a hostage in a culture that was hostile to his faith. The message of Daniel, then, is not that God will remove all forms of oppression in our lives. Instead, this account serves as a reminder that when you know Heaven rules, you can find success and remain faithful to Him despite the most trying of circumstances.

And even in the midst of great wickedness, you can be known as a person of great godliness. Daniel lived in a society that was utterly pagan and yet there is not a negative word about him in the entire Bible. When the leaders of Babylon tried to uncover some fault in his life, they found nothing worthy of mention except his faith in God (Dan. 6:4–5). Daniel was living on earth, but he had set his affections on things above. God in heaven was ruling his life.

Through all the plots and intrigues that regularly lurked in royal courts, through all the jealousy that could only be expected toward a foreigner in high office, through all the envy, conspiracies, and persecutions, Daniel continued to serve his God without wavering. God in heaven was ruling his life on earth!

It is likely that Daniel influenced as many as thirteen kings and four kingdoms in his lifetime. Wicked as most of these kings were, Daniel's counsel, courage, and absolute integrity often turned them away from idolatry and caused them to recognize the power of the true God.

As Nancy Wolgemuth tells this story, she goes out of her way to bring it home to us with illustrations from modern-day people who today are living through their own challenging experiences and affirming that "Heaven rules."

In other words, Heaven rules, even when your unborn child dies. Heaven rules when you find out that your husband of many years has been unfaithful to you. Heaven rules when tornados destroy everything you've spent your entire life building. Heaven rules when you stand up for your faith as a godly football coach and get fired for doing so. According to Nancy,

> "Heaven rules" means He is sovereign over everything
> that touches us. . . . He is ruler over every diagnosis and

prognosis, over all incomes and outcomes, over the most daunting challenges as well as the most seemingly trivial details of our lives.

Several years ago, as I began to be asked to write forewords and endorsements for books, I determined that I would never endorse a book I had not fully read. So, I want to report to you that I have read every word of this book. In fact, I have read some of these words multiple times. At first, I read just to find out what the book was all about. But about thirty pages into the manuscript I felt my spirit lifted and my heart encouraged. I was really being blessed. I couldn't wait to tell my wife and some of my close friends about the powerful message of this book.

I hope you will do as I have done and read every word and then remind the people you know and love that "Heaven rules."

DR. DAVID JEREMIAH
Senior Pastor, Shadow Mountain Community Church
Founder and host, Turning Point Radio and Television Ministries

Samuel's Story

Saturday, June 12, 2021

KATIE BOLLINGER was doing some of the few things a pregnant woman can do when she's two days short of being forty weeks along. She spent the morning swinging with her three other "littles" and snuggling with them around her belly, trying to fill up their love buckets with special attention. Always a mom, she wanted to do everything possible to help with their adjustment to a new baby in the house—a new baby brother, Katie and Nathan's second son. They knew it was a boy. In fact, they'd already given him a name: Samuel Ethan.

Finally, late in the afternoon, Katie was able to find a quiet enough spot in her day to lie down and take the weight off her swollen calves and ankles. Usually when she'd stretch out that way, she could feel the baby doing the same, as if glad to be given the extra space. She wasn't sure she felt him doing it right then, but hey, there wasn't really much space left there for him to find! Katie drifted into sleep thinking about little Samuel, eager to see him, looking forward to finally holding him.

Yet even as she was slowly awakening an hour or so later, she realized the baby still wasn't moving. A chill shuddered through her body. Was she imagining it? Surely he was fine.

She got up and ate a little something, a granola bar. ("It's crazy how sugar makes babies move!" Katie says). No movement. She lay down and stretched out again. Still nothing. She couldn't feel Samuel kicking at all.

Nathan called his parents, who live nearby, and asked if they could come over to watch the other children so he and Katie could head to the hospital, just to check, to be sure the baby was okay. Once at the childbirth unit, they were taken to a triage room. With Nathan at his wife's side, holding her hand, the nurse placed a monitor on Katie's belly. They listened for the familiar strong heartbeat, but all they heard was silence. A loud, throbbing silence.

Nathan texted a handful of close friends to share what they had just learned:

> Please pray for us! We just went into the hospital to check on our baby boy. Samuel Ethan Bollinger is in Jesus' hands. The doctor confirmed that there is no heartbeat. We will communicate more soon as we are able. Katie will be induced soon.

Within a short time Katie found herself in labor, then deep into the delivery process. Nearly twenty-four hours later Samuel came, all eight pounds and ten ounces of him, just one day short of when he'd been due to arrive. But now grief filled the room where gladness and celebration were supposed to be.

It was the hardest day, the hardest moment, that Katie and Nathan had ever endured.

Sunday, June 13, 4:33 p.m.

. . .

The Bollingers have been friends and ministry colleagues of mine for over a decade. Along with the rest of our team at Revive Our Hearts, I had watched God bring their lives together and then grace them with three precious children. The reality of this devastating news stung at a deep place for those of us who had rejoiced with them at the news of this fourth child and had eagerly awaited his birth. We felt crushed for them. With them.

For years I've opened God's Word and taught that things don't "just happen," that our God is in control. He knows what He's doing. The events that touch our lives are purposeful. It's a truth that runs all through the Scripture. But then a moment like this comes along, when it's so painfully hard to understand. Can this biblical belief, this anchored truth, offer comfort and courage to someone who is right in the middle of life's worst?

Another incoming text interrupted my thoughts and prayers that night. This one came from Nathan's mom, an update on the situation at the hospital. Embedded beneath her few words was a picture Nathan had sent her of a whiteboard. You've seen these in hospital rooms. You know: nurse and doctor names, contact numbers, instructive messages, all written and erased a thousand times.

Across the top of the board in the room where Katie was still in labor, one new message, printed by Nathan with a red marker, was impossible to miss:

Heaven rules!
And Samuel is there!!

Seeing that image and inscription on my phone took my breath away. It was a sacred moment for me—as it was for those in that grief-filled hospital room. Katie later wrote and told me she'd read those words "hundreds of times" during the labor process. "It helped reframe my perspective on a continually needed basis," she said. "It's been amazing to see how God has gone before us and given us truths to cling to."

You see, over the previous three weeks, Nathan had been the video producer helping to record a teaching series for the Revive Our Hearts podcast. During these recordings I walked through the book of Daniel, looking at each chapter through the lens of its proclamation that "Heaven rules." (Yes, the podcast was the genesis of this book.) So over the course of those sessions, I must have repeated the phrase dozens of times.

From his position seated in the control room, watching the sessions on monitors, Nathan had taken in this teaching, which was already deeply imprinted in his and Katie's hearts. He had listened to me introduce this series by reminding the audience that

God is sovereign over rulers, over nations, over geopolitical affairs in our world. He is also sovereign over the events and the happenings and the details in our individual lives. It's true even when the script turns out far different than what we would have written if the pen had been in our hands. . . .

"Heaven rules" is not a trite thought. This is not a throwaway line. This is huge! And this is what will anchor your heart when you're being tossed and thrown in the storms of life.[1]

Now, back in that hospital room, my precious friends were in the middle of the storm of their lives. The loss, too fresh to quite believe and absorb, was raw, aching, gripping. The hours of intense labor only to deliver a fully formed, lifeless baby. The FaceTime call to tell Samuel's siblings that the little brother they had been so excited to meet was in heaven and would not be coming home. Then the couple of hours in the hospital room with parents, grandparents, and small sisters and brother each having a chance to hold Samuel's body.

It was too fragile a moment to want to touch.

Yet as Katie and Nathan described in a poignant "letter to Samuel" several days later, "That delivery room was a holy ground of worship amidst the deepest of heartache."

Worship? Intermingled with weeping? Yes.

My husband and I joined hundreds of heartbroken friends

for Samuel's service. You never forget those kinds of funerals. Robert and I sat among the other mourners, heavy tears pooling at the corners of our eyes, transfixed on the tiny casket resting at the front of the church.

The hush in the sanctuary expressed unspoken words in our hearts: *How can this precious couple and their children just go home and go on with their lives, having held death in their arms, having seen it in the face of their sweet little son, of their tiny brother?*

And then the service began—with worship. With singing, exalting the High King of heaven.

On the front row stood the bereaved couple, with their three children and two sets of grandparents on either side of them, their eyes, hands, and voices lifted to heaven. In worship.

The letter Katie and Nathan had written to their son was read by their pastor during the funeral. It was a stunning statement of faith, declaring God's goodness and Heaven's rule, and included these tender words:

> Our precious Samuel Ethan. Your first name means "God has heard," and your middle name means "strong, safe." We had no idea, when God led us to that name, how perfect it would be for you! You are now completely strong and safe in the arms of God, who heard our prayers.

Underneath these unplanned, tragic circumstances, support-ing and carrying this sorrowing family, stood the One whose

reign over every situation—and I do mean *every* situation—
could take even *this* situation to its knees in worship.

Heaven rules!
And Samuel is there!!

Heaven rules, and there is nowhere He is not.

Comforting us. Giving us courage.

Through our tears, through our fears, calling and leading us
to worship.

CHAPTER ONE

A Single Lens

The sovereignty of God is the one impregnable rock
to which the suffering human heart must cling.

—Margaret Clarkson

IF ONLY THE KING had believed the truth years earlier. The truth
might have kept him from going crazy.

It's what keeps any of us from going crazy.

• • •

Tucked away toward the end of your Old Testament is a small-
ish book you may have checked off in your Bible reading plan
more than once without ever pausing to dig deeper into its message. The narrative portions of the book of Daniel are familiar
enough to many that it's tempting to gloss over them. Perhaps
you've heard these stories since childhood, as I have. Interwoven
through those accounts are a number of complex dreams and
visions, along with some of the most detailed prophecies found
in the Bible. These portions seem incomprehensible at points,

making it easy to skip over them in favor of passages that make more sense to us.

I hope you won't, however, because the book of Daniel has so much to say to us.

The characters, historical details, and timelines we encounter in this little book may appear to be archaic, confusing, and relatively insignificant, especially against the backdrop of events that loom large in our world today. But this inspired record—both the well-known stories and the prophetic maze that winds its way through them—could not be more relevant or timely for your life and mine.

Take, for example, a striking scene found in Daniel 4, in which we come across the two words that I chose for the title for this book—the words that touched all of us so deeply on the occasion of baby Samuel's death:

Heaven rules.

No phrase pulses more frequently in my mind and heart than this one. It's on the screensaver photo that pops up every time I look at my phone. It's printed on the mug I use each morning for my tea. It's featured on artwork hanging in my study. It's engraved on a gold necklace hanging around my neck, a gift from a dear friend who is battling terminal cancer.

"Heaven rules" is a right-sizing truth—putting our view of God, our view of ourselves, and our view of our problems in proper perspective.

I love being surrounded by reminders of this simple but profound truth. It has become for me an overarching, undergirding meta-theme, foundational to how I view all of Scripture and all of life. And over and over again, when I have found myself in tumultuous waters, it has been both an anchor and a life preserver for my soul.

As you read what follows, I pray that these two words will take hold of you and that they will stay with you long after you've closed this book and returned it to the shelf. My hope is that the promise and the perspective contained in the phrase

> ∧
> "Heaven rules" is a right-sizing truth—putting our view of God, our view of ourselves, and our view of our problems in proper perspective.
> ∨

will become deeply and forever ingrained in the fabric of your being, that it will bring you comfort and courage in every painful season and perplexing circumstance of your life, and that it will become your reflexive, trusting response to every crisis and troubling development in our upside-down world.

THE KING AND HIS DREAM

Now, travel back with me to the sixth century BC, to the capital of the vast, sprawling Babylonian empire, as we make our way into the palace where we will meet a powerful man who was forced to learn the hard way that Heaven rules. He tells the story himself in Daniel 4, years after it happened to him.

You'll get the most out of this book if you read it with your Bible opened to the book of Daniel. In fact, before moving on, let me encourage you to take a few minutes to read Daniel 4. As you read, highlight each reference to God as "the Most High." And ask yourself: What did the Babylonian king's life look like before—and after—he acknowledged Heaven's rule?

Flush with success and renowned for his legendary accomplishments and military exploits, Nebuchadnezzar, the reigning monarch, experienced a distressing dream. He instantly recognized that it possessed significant meaning—that it was not just the quirky remains of an unprocessed memory from earlier in the day. But he didn't know what that meaning was until he consulted the prophet Daniel, known as the wise man Belteshazzar in his court.

In the dream Nebuchadnezzar had seen a tree—a tall, towering, massive tree, lush and full, beautiful and abundant. Happy birds and forest animals had come from all over the earth to sleep under it, eat from it, and nest within its branches, deriving nourishing pleasure from its fruit and shade. This tree, as he now learned from Daniel, was a visual image of Nebuchadnezzar himself, the most powerful and influential figure in the known world at the time.

But the scene with the awe-inspiring tree had suddenly been shattered by the loud, commanding appearance of an angel soaring down from the sky and shouting out an order to "cut down the tree and chop off its branches," to "strip off its leaves and scatter its fruit," leaving nothing but the stump and its roots in the ground—a shocking blow to the king's mighty strength and standing.

Worse, the angel had described the tree-king descending into madness, being "drenched with dew from the sky," pawing wildly at the ground for food, his mind changed "from that of a human" to that "of an animal" (Dan. 4:14–16).

And it happened! The events the dream foretold took place just as the angel had described and Daniel had interpreted to Nebuchadnezzar. What a comedown—from hero to zero. From universal acclaim to utter humiliation. Stripped of prestige and power. Reduced to grinding out an existence as a brute beast.

Why? To what purpose was this dramatic takedown? As Nebuchadnezzar recounted his memories of this whole series of events—the dream itself, the prophet's warning, a year's reprieve, then seven years of insanity—he remembered well the "why," having heard it spoken more than once throughout his long ordeal:

> "This is so that the living will know that the Most High is ruler." (4:17)

> "The Most High is ruler." (4:25)

> "The Most High is ruler." (4:32)

Or, as Daniel had declared when explaining the meaning of the dream to the king:

> "Your kingdom will be restored to you as soon as you acknowledge that *Heaven rules*." (4:26)

Yes, the sooner we know and believe this truth, the saner we all can be.

CORRECTION, COMFORT, AND COURAGE

The seeds for this book were first planted in my heart in 2020. Who could ever forget 2020? It was a sad, unsettling, disturbing year. A crazy-feeling year. The news about the COVID-19 pandemic became a daily drip—both fatiguing and frightful. And the stress it created spread to other elements of our society: polarized politics, racial tensions, underlying distrust of government and the news media, and embittered disagreements along partisan lines. Even families, churches, and longtime friendships felt the splintering effects.

And the turmoil was hardly limited to the United States. Economies staggered throughout the world, unemployment soared, public dissension exploded, political and social issues festered. Wave after wave of crises—many COVID related, others not—came crashing in upon the shores of our collective emotions and values, until every day felt as though the sky was falling. This tree of civilization we'd been growing—so proud, so expansively self-assured, so illustrious in appearance and in its representation of the kingdom of man—was being shaken to its roots by the might of another kingdom. Another Ruler.

Yes, whether we recognize it or not, whether we concur or not, the truth remains:

Heaven rules.

By "Heaven rules," of course, I mean "God rules." The God of heaven rules. He rules over every tide of history, over every king and kingdom, over every activity we undertake, over every person and part of His creation. "Heaven rules" is a right-sizing truth—putting our view of God, our view of ourselves, and our view of our problems in proper perspective. It's a truth meant to instill healthy fear within every proud heart that aims to be its own ruler and that believes we humans can determine our own direction and destiny.

That's how Heaven's rule *corrects* us, and we're crazy to think we don't need it. God is kind, not cruel, in reminding us who's in charge and in doing it at whatever cost He knows is necessary to get our distracted attention. None of us really wants to find out what would happen if He weren't in charge!

> He is ruler over every diagnosis and prognosis, over all incomes and outcomes, over the most daunting challenges as well as the most seemingly trivial details of our lives.

But here's why I've written this book. This same truth that corrects us is also intended to *comfort* us. To reassure and free us. To catch us and keep us. "Heaven rules" means He is sovereign over everything that touches us, that nothing comes to us unbidden by His desire to use it for our good and for His glory and for the greater things He created us to be part of. He is ruler over every diagnosis and prognosis, over all incomes and outcomes, over the most daunting challenges as well as the most seemingly trivial details of our lives.

This truth that is powerful enough to take down the great is also powerful enough to bear up the least of us, both in our private ordeals and as we face the world that seems to be imploding around us. We can take comfort as we walk on this earth because of our Father's rule from heaven. Comfort and *courage*—for "Heaven rules" does not call for a passive acceptance of fate; it comes with the promise of grace for the battle. When we feel we just can't withstand any more pressure, problems, or pain, the awareness of God's rule infuses us with supernatural strength. It enables us to live with contented, cemented clarity through the chaos and the ugly fallout of a fallen world, through struggles and circumstances that make us want to run away in panic or curl up in despair. We find the courage to patiently, even joyfully, persevere in the assurance that Heaven rules.

Not even 2020 could topple this truth.

Throughout that year, however, my husband and I were tested to find out if we really believed it to be true.

First, a bit of background. As perhaps you know, in 2015 a widower named Robert Wolgemuth asked this fifty-seven-year-old, never-married woman to marry him. I said, "Yes, with all my heart." Of the many experiences I've had in my life that testify to Heaven's rule, one that's up there near the top is God's providential plan for leading me into marriage with this precious man.

Less than five years after we said "I do," the Lord led us into another major opportunity to experience and embrace His sovereign rule in our lives. Just as the world was being upended by the global pandemic, my otherwise healthy husband, over the course of just a handful of months, received diagnoses of two—that's right, *two*—different, unrelated cancers.

As you'd imagine—or perhaps you know all too well from firsthand experience—the arrival of this invasive unknown brought with it waves of sadness. Unspoken fears. Hard, tearful conversations. Long waits for critical test results and for clear information on what to expect next.

And as you have found to be the case in difficult chapters of your own story, we had a choice to make.

> /\
> We can take comfort
> as we walk on this earth
> because of our Father's
> rule from heaven.
> Comfort and *courage*...
> to patiently, even joyfully,
> persevere.
> \/

Not regarding whether our lives were to be impacted by cancer—we were not given an option about that. The question was how we would receive and respond to this new reality. How we would prepare ourselves to endure it and begin walking through it, having no way of knowing the ups and downs to come—or even if "down" was the only direction it would take us.

We can take comfort as we walk on this earth because of our

Father's rule from heaven. Comfort and *courage* . . . to patiently, even joyfully, persevere.

Looking back, we can see clearly that God had been preparing us for this journey. In 2019, before the arrival of either COVID or cancer-times-two, Robert and I coauthored a book we called *You Can Trust God to Write Your Story: Embracing the Mysteries of Providence.* In one chapter we reflected on God's providences— some painful, some beautiful, but all good—in our own story. At the end of that chapter we wrote,

> We can't help but wonder what rocky paths we may yet
> be called to travel. . . . We may yet face serious health
> issues, losing one or the other to death, and/or other
> crises known only to Him. But we know He has been
> faithful in each chapter thus far. And we know that He
> will be faithful in each one yet to come, that His grace
> will be sufficient for wherever He leads us.[1]

We maintained, in other words, as Scripture does, that God could be trusted to write our story. And in 2020 we held to that belief, even when double cancer showed up in a leading role as antagonist.

To put it more succinctly, we knew that Heaven rules.

How I have come to cling to these two words from Daniel's long-ago conversation with the Babylonian king. And how I have grown to love them. In fact, if you were to look through my Bible or through my journals, texts, emails, and stray pieces of paper scattered throughout my home and study, you might see scribbled here and there two letters that have become part of the warp and woof of my life:

HR

"Heaven rules." I can't recall a time when I didn't know and believe this theological truth at some level, thanks to parents who taught and lived it out in our home as I was growing up. But increasingly, throughout my adulthood and even more so in recent years, this way of viewing the complexities and crises of life in this broken world has captured my heart. It has become a lens through which I see and process, well, *everything.* Rarely does a day go by when I don't speak of it or share it in some fashion with someone else, some person who's gasping for air amid the churning white water of their own worries or questions or fears or difficulties. Just minutes ago, in fact, I had occasion to remind a dear friend of this reassuring truth in a phone conversation.

"Heaven rules," to me, is not some nebulous adage confined to the unseen realms beyond time and space. It reminds us that our God in heaven is actively controlling and working through every single happening, event, and circumstance taking place on the earth, and He is doing it to accomplish His good, eternal, redemptive purposes.

He is doing it despite whatever you may hear concerning the state of our world while watching or scrolling through the news of the day.

He is doing it despite whatever pops up as you check your email or social media feeds after you emerge from a long meeting.

He is doing it despite the nervousness that's ticking under your wristwatch while you're perched in yet another doctor's office or hospital waiting room, listening for your name to be called.

Heaven is still ruling. Heaven is *always* ruling.

I realize it doesn't always seem that way. It may appear, at times, that just the opposite is true. On any given news day, it can feel like our world is spinning out of control, that evildoers are winning the day, and that God is helpless (or unwilling) to do anything about it.

As I write this chapter, our news feeds are being flooded with reports of havoc and even genocide taking place in Ukraine. Does Heaven rule in this corner of the world that is being reduced to rubble?

On a more personal level, it may seem that God is dismissive toward your situation, sluggish to act, even coldly unconcerned about matters weighing heavily on your mind and heart, difficulties that distract and distress you and sabotage your joy.

But for those who "know their God" (Dan. 11:32), not even the most dreaded, drastic, or deathly occurrences can steal their hope and confidence in Him. All will be well, even though at the moment nothing seems to be well. This truth is unshakable, despite any and all indications to the contrary. Even when storms are raging within and around us, you and I can sleep in peace each night, and each morning we can awaken to renewed comfort and courage because of this immutable, irrefutable reality.

Because Heaven rules.

LIVING PROOF

In the midst of all the upheaval that came with 2020, with the disruptions we were all experiencing from COVID and unsettling cultural issues, as well as those Robert and I were facing more personally with his cancer, I found myself drawn anew to the book of Daniel. What I discovered there gave me the fresh, daily hope and perspective that I desperately needed.

Daniel was among the first generation of Jewish citizens who were deported from their home in Judah by Babylon's king, Nebuchadnezzar, who took Jerusalem around 605 BC. Some scholars think young Daniel was no more than fourteen years old when he first appeared in the book bearing his name. I find this especially interesting, because if Daniel's responses had been driven by circumstances and surroundings, as is so often the case with teens (adults too!), he easily could have concluded that God had abandoned him along with the rest of his people. Why else had they been forcibly relocated to Babylon against their will?

But the compelling testimony of Daniel's entire life is that Heaven rules despite all appearances to the contrary. The best-known events in this short book attest to this truth:

- Daniel being strategically placed in position, as a Hebrew in a foreign land, to interpret King Nebuchadnezzar's dreams (Dan. 2 and 4)
- Daniel's three young friends (Shadrach, Meshach, and Abednego) being thrown into a fiery furnace for refusing to bow to Nebuchadnezzar's statue (Dan. 3)

- another Babylonian king, Belshazzar, whose collapse from power occurred in a single night, being informed of his imminent downfall by the chilling appearance of a disembodied handwriting on the palace wall (Dan. 5)
- and, of course, the most well-known story of them all: Daniel being thrown into the lions' den (Dan. 6)

These accounts, which span roughly seven decades, can be found in the first half of the book of Daniel. They add up to a life that was beyond remarkable.

The second half of his book, however, is less familiar to most. It contains a host of cryptic prophetic clues about the impending fall of the Babylonian empire, as well as the rise of as-yet-unknown empires that God was positioning to emerge in subsequent centuries. These events would set the stage for the eventual advent of God's Messiah—the coming of Christ to earth—at the Lord's appointed time, as well as His ultimate reign over an eternal kingdom that has no end (Dan. 7–12). The prophetic view that emerges is fascinating, glorious, and not always easy to understand.

Years ago, when I was in Bible college, a popular (though difficult) course offered each year was "Daniel/Revelation." It explored and attempted to make sense of the ins and outs of these two colossal prophetic books, one in the Old Testament, the other in the New. With the guidance of a knowledgeable Bible professor, students set out to decipher this apocalyptic literature, much of it shrouded in symbolism, attempting to determine what was supposed to happen when in the yet-unknown future.

To be sure, there's a place for that kind of academic effort. But in this book I want us to step back and consider the book of Daniel (as we could also do with the book of Revelation) through a single lens—the lens of "Heaven rules."

Now, in no way does the affirmation of Heaven's rule suggest that Daniel's life was charmed and easy. It was anything but. From his teenage years until the end of his life, he spent his days in exile, far from his homeland. He lived and worked for roughly seventy years under multiple kings, faithfully serving his God under the godless rulers of successive world powers. He faced temptations and trials galore, being forced repeatedly to choose between his faith in his God (whom he knew as the "Most High") and the whims of pagan despots and administrations. The political terrain never stopped shifting beneath his feet, even as the peril of being fed to a pride of hungry lions, both literally and figuratively, encircled him.

Yet Daniel's calm, humble, prayerful confidence in the Lord not only kept him upright (except when he knelt to pray) but also made him a sought-out voice of reason in times of crisis. He outlasted one king and regime change after another, not by ranting and railing against evil powers, not by protesting against the wicked systems they perpetuated, but by holding fast to an unchangeable fact: earthly rulers rise and fall, but the Most High God is never in danger of being removed from His throne, and He will never abandon the people He calls His own.

Throughout his long, storied life, Daniel remained a stalwart pillar of faith, exerting a righteous influence in an unrighteous environment. This is due to the fact that he fixed his sight on the long view—the certainty of God's everlasting kingdom—even as he faced the unpredictable headwinds caused by an endless succession of dysfunctional leaders and anti-God governments.

Can you see why the account given to us in the book of Daniel is so applicable and needed today? Here where we live and serve in the "Babylon" we know—whether it be in my homeland of America or elsewhere in the world—the life, words, and demeanor of this faithful, faith-filled man provide a model for believers in our own day and for those of every generation.

That's why I don't consider it any coincidence that the Lord in His providence turned my attention to Daniel's story in Scripture as my own world (and perhaps your world, certainly *the* world) was roiling and seizing. Through that intense period, as I soaked in the book of Daniel, the truth of "Heaven rules" proved to be bracing to me, a solid rock for my faith. The things God taught me and showed me through Daniel have caused this phrase to become my true north in an even richer, sweeter way then I had ever experienced before. And today, when life and the world so often feel upside down, this exquisite, enduring truth keeps me right side up.

"Heaven rules" is how Robert and I, by God's daily, enabling grace, are seeking to face all of life. Mercifully, as I'm writing today, we are looking at cancer through the rearview mirror, although the journey has entailed more surgical procedures, blood transfusions, needle sticks, chemo treatments, biopsies, scans, and hospital stays than we thought our two calendars (and one man's body!) could possibly accommodate. You just make room when Heaven rules.

But even with the sense of relief we're currently feeling on that front, we still must deliberately choose to trust and praise God each day, regardless of what He apportions to us in His all-good, all-wise design for our lives. Our confidence as we wait for Him to unfold our next season remains the same today as it was back in 2019, in that pre-COVID, pre-cancer season, when we wrote:

> As we sit here today, we have no idea what our future may hold. Our story is still being written, and He has not given us an inside track on what the next chapters look like. But our trust is in the One who holds our future . . . [who] gives us freedom and peace, even when we cannot see what lies ahead.[2]

Heaven rules. It really is true. And no threat, no problem, whether in our own little world or in the great big world around us, can ever steal that assurance from us.

THE VALUE OF A SINGLE LENS

We all know what it is to feel outweighed by life and bewildered when faced with hard things, especially unexpected things. Life just gives us a lot to think about. To worry about.

For this reason, my goal in this book is to fix our hearts on *one single truth*, one that applies to every episode, every piece and particle, of our lives and times. It's an outlook that takes the randomness and apparent impossibility out of each moment, translating it instead into an opportunity to get a clearer view of this God we serve and worship, an opportunity for that God to be seen and made real to those around us.

There's value in seeing things through a single lens.

I don't know a lot about photography—beyond taking pictures with my cell phone—but I know that most serious photographers today use what's called a single-lens reflex camera (SLR).

The single-lens camera, as I've had it explained to me, was a significant breakthrough in camera technology when it first came on the market, primarily because of one innovation. Other camera styles in use at the time required the photographer to look through a viewfinder positioned above or to the side of the lens rather than through the lens itself. And so, no matter how long or how carefully you stared at the object in view, the best you could do was guess at what the picture would ultimately look like. Because the real picture wasn't what you saw in the viewfinder. The real picture was only on the other side of that lens, where reality lived. Where the real picture was happening.

You and I, in looking at what's going on in our world, in our home, in our relationships, or in our bodies, have a variety of viewfinder options we can choose from, different ways of trying to perceive and interpret what we're seeing, to imagine where all of it is going and why. But though we inevitably "see through a glass darkly," as Scripture tells us (1 Cor. 13:12 KJV), we will see a lot more clearly if our eyes are on what's actually taking place, not on the many earthly, temporal viewpoints masquerading as what matters most.

And here's what truly matters: Heaven rules.

HR

Put that picture on your wall and see if it doesn't bring a new focus to your whole life.

A PRESENT FROM THE FUTURE

Let's go back to the story of Nebuchadnezzar that opened this chapter. This fiercely independent ruler who fancied himself master of his own fate needed to come face to face with the fact that he was utterly at the mercy of the God of heaven. And Daniel told him just that.

After explaining that the dream about the luxuriant tree being cut down was a warning to the proud king, Daniel earnestly appealed to him and offered hope if he would humble himself and repent: "Separate yourself from your sins by doing what is right. . . . Perhaps there will be an extension of your prosperity" (Dan. 4:27).

God gave Nebuchadnezzar ample opportunity—a whole year after the dream (4:29)—to bow before Heaven's rule. But when he persisted in his delusion of autonomy and self-grandeur, God deposed him from his throne and left him to rummage for food on his hands and knees like a soulless animal.

Seven years later, the once-arrogant king of Babylon had finally come to see life through a completely different lens. "At the end of those days," he said, "I . . . looked up to heaven, and my sanity returned to me" (4:34). Finally. He'd wasted all those years pushing back against what the angel and Daniel had said about the Most High being ruler. And yet all these years later, the truth was still the same. It was right where the truth had always been. Right where the truth always is. Just waiting for an ancient king, or maybe the person we see in the mirror each day, to "acknowledge that Heaven rules."

Heaven ruled then.

Heaven rules today.

Heaven will rule tomorrow.

And Heaven will rule through all eternity.

How much better, rather than living seven—or more—years in unnecessary, self-inflicted turmoil and humiliation, if we just go ahead and live now inside the comfort and courage of God's forever rule. It's where the future meets the present. Where His omnipotence meets our frailty. Where comfort meets courage. And where nobody ever has to go crazy in the process.

CHAPTER TWO

The Story behind the Story

God is always doing 10,000 things in your life,
and you may be aware of three of them.

—John Piper

THE STORY OF DANIEL takes place in the context of the Babylonian captivity—when the Jewish people endured seventy years of exile in Babylon under the iron fist of a tyrannical despot. The experience was brutal. Harrowing. Exhausting. Seemingly endless. And pointless.

That's what God's chosen people could see. That's what it felt like from their vantage point.

And that's what our story and our world sometimes look and feel like to us. Proud people and senseless policies. Devaluing and disrespecting what we hold dear. Wearing us out with their never-ending assaults on truth and those who treasure it. And don't forget that tireless enemy of God and His people, the devil himself, inserting himself into the goings-on of this world and exerting the fullest extent of whatever (limited) powers he possesses to wreak havoc in every direction.

It's all vexing and wearying, to say the least.

But above and beyond all that we see and experience here on earth is a far different, far greater story unfolding. And *that* story would become clear to us if only we could see life's happenings and hardships from heaven's perspective.

Take, for example, a story that began against the backdrop of cruelties carried out in the Soviet Union in the first half of the twentieth century. To those who were victimized by these events, the visible realities were harsh and inexplicable. But as it turned out, the painful happenings that could be seen here on earth were setting the stage for a greater, unseen, redemptive story God was writing from heaven.

(Just a heads up: this account is a bit complex to follow; but it's worth the effort. It beautifully illustrates an important principle we'll find at work in the book of Daniel—as well as in our own stories, if our spiritual eyes are open to see it.)

. . .

In late October 1937, just as winter was tightening its icy grip on the northern latitudes of Russia, trains of rail cars began rolling out of the farthest eastern regions of its vast territory. Each compartment was packed with ethnic Koreans being deported from the only home their families had known since the late 1800s.[1]

The Russians had first acquired this largely uninhabited land area from China during the days of the Qing dynasty, seeking an ice-free Pacific port for trade and naval vessels. Desiring also a geographical buffer between themselves and Japan, the Russians had sought to befriend the Korean migrants who had already begun resettling there after severe famines drove them northward and had arrived in greater numbers when Japan moved into Korea.

But by 1937 Russia had gathered a number of neighbor states into the massive United Soviet Socialist Republics. Joseph Stalin had established himself as dictator of the USSR. And Stalin, much like Hitler, saw enemies of the state everywhere he looked. Though these Koreans living in Russia's easternmost regions were nothing of the sort, he suspected them of either harboring or functioning as spies, and he arbitrarily ordered their exile deep into Central Asia—four thousand miles away!

The numbers vary, but best guesses put the size of the Korean deportation at 170,000 souls, possibly more. They arrived in the Soviet satellite states now known as Uzbekistan and Kazakhstan, where they were now forbidden from practicing their long-held traditions. Their children were taught the Russian language in school. In time, these Korean nationals would become absorbed into the culture around them, though they were treated as second-class citizens and forced to suffer the indignities of prejudice and racial bias.

Again, the deportation happened in 1937.

Now, fast-forward fifty years. By the late 1980s the Soviet Union, which for decades had stood nose-to-nose against the United States in the titanic standoff known as the Cold War, began to show signs of cracking. In a desperate attempt to save their faltering Communist system, the Soviets, led by Mikhail Gorbachev, initiated efforts to remake some of their economic policies (*perestroika*) and to open their closed society to the world (a principle called *glasnost*).[2]

It was all over the news. Everybody was talking about the pending breakup of the Soviet Union. It seemed impossible— almost hopeful, yet still more than a little frightening, given the history of US-Soviet relations. The two had been at each other's throats for so long, battling to see which side would ultimately prevail. What would happen next? Would the drastic changes contribute to world peace or dangerous destabilization?

For our purposes here, let's call this the view from *earth's perspective*.

Meanwhile, as the Soviet states of Central Asia were beginning to open their doors to foreign interests, the church in South Korea was experiencing explosive, unprecedented growth. Though persecuted and suppressed by their Japanese overlords throughout the first half of the twentieth century, the church had emerged from the Korean War years (1950–1953) into a period of vibrant growth. And as it grew, so did its zeal for sending out missionaries to evangelize people in other lands.

The evolving situation in the former Soviet Union proved especially intriguing. Korean missionaries, like others, were eager to take advantage of this new opening, which included the now independent states of Uzbekistan and Kazakhstan. When these missionaries arrived, they were faced with the expected cross-cultural challenges of trying to reach people with whom they shared no history or background—except for the fact that there among the Uzbeks and Kazakhs were hundreds of thousands of people who for generations had been living as Russians but who were obviously of Korean descent.

Suddenly—surprisingly?—these South Korean missionaries found themselves surrounded by third- and fourth-generation Koreans who, despite having their ancestral roots chopped out from beneath them by Stalin's actions against their grandparents and great-grandparents in 1937, seemed quite interested in reacquiring cultural ties with their traditional homeland. As a result, these missionaries found fertile ground for sowing seeds of the gospel. And because of the thorough assimilation of these Korean expats into local society, they were also able to gain inroads through them to the hearts of many others in the region.

This story wasn't what we were hearing on the nightly newscasts of the early 1990s or reading about in our morning newspapers. And yet, in the cold, cramped quarters of those dilapidated train cars rattling across the unforgiving Russian landscape, seemingly abandoned by the living God who supposedly made the world and ruled everything in it, this very God had been invisibly at work, writing a story and enacting a plan that would not be seen and known on earth for decades to come. An eternal, redemptive plan, through which many thousands would be brought to bow the knee before Christ.

Let's call this the view from *heaven's perspective.*

Because in any situation, no matter how it looks from the earth, there's another story behind the story. There is heaven's side of the story. And this story—viewed from heaven's vantage point—is just as real, even more real, than how things appear to most observers here on earth. There's what you can see happening here on earth, and there's what God is doing from heaven that we may not be able to see or realize at the time.

As we walk together through Daniel's story, keep a look out for these two different perspectives. Don't be afraid to mark up the passages we'll consider, as I've done in my Bible. Make a note when you see what's happening from earth's point of view. And when you get a glimpse of God's engagement and intervention, you may want to write "*HR*" (*Heaven rules*) in the margin.

Start by taking a few minutes to read Daniel 1. As you review this opening narrative, ask: What was going on from *earth's* perspective? And: What was *God* doing behind the scenes in the midst of these events? Make a note of any *HR* sightings.

BEHIND THE HEADLINES

The book of Daniel opens in "the third year of the reign of King Jehoiakim of Judah," when "King Nebuchadnezzar of Babylon came to Jerusalem and laid siege to it" (Dan. 1:1).

There you have it—the timestamp and the historical context for the events that follow.

This is the kind of report you'll see and hear in the news today. Crisp, concise, clear journalism giving names, dates, and human actions.

The forces of Babylon came to Jerusalem and encircled its outer walls, cutting off its supply chain. That's exactly what happened.

But this abbreviated account leaves out a key piece of information. It does what journalists call "burying the lede." It overlooks the main thrust or importance of the story by focusing entirely on the obvious details. All trees, no forest.

> In any situation, no matter how it looks from the earth, there's another story behind the story. There is heaven's side of the story.

The perspective that's missing in the first verse of Daniel 1—the perspective that matters most—is found in the next verse, where the Bible reports not only the historic takeover of the city, the land, and its king[3] but also makes it clear who was doing what:

> *The Lord* handed King Jehoiakim of Judah over to [Nebuchadnezzar]. (Dan. 1:2)

There's your story. It's God, the subject of every sentence. God, the active hand behind every happening. (Hint: this is a good place to jot down "HR" in your Bible.)

We've already referenced the two important theological terms related to this concept: God's *sovereignty* and God's *providence.* Their meanings are somewhat similar, but each is distinct enough that together they paint for us an even broader sweep of what God does and why He does it.

- *Sovereignty* means His right as Creator to rule over His creation.
- *Providence* refers to the ways He uses His sovereign power to accomplish His purposes.
- *Sovereignty* means we belong to Him and He can do with us whatever He wants.
- *Providence* says He acts in ways that advance His good, wise plan for us.

So there's sovereignty, and there's providence. Deity with design. Power with purpose. It's not enough just to say that things happen for a reason; the point is that things happen for *God's* reasons. God Himself is actively at work in our world and in our lives to carry out His own objectives.

This reality is woven throughout Scripture. For instance:

> The Lord does whatever he pleases
> in heaven and on earth. (Ps. 135:6)

That's God's *sovereignty.* And:

> [He] works out everything in agreement with the
> purpose of his will. (Eph. 1:11)

That's God's *providence.*

Will we always understand what God is doing in the world and in our lives? Of course not. We're not God. But here's what we can be sure of. Put together, God's sovereignty (His entitlement) and His providence (His intentional intervention, which

Romans 8:28 says is always good toward His people) are able to shield you and me and our often-quaking hearts inside an impenetrable fortress.

This tells us that even in those hard, scary places of life—such as when God's people, including Daniel, were captured and carried away from their homeland to a hostile environment—there's more to what's going on than just what can be seen from earth's perspective. There's another way of looking at it, a heavenly perspective.

And though earth's happenings often seem random, meaningless, hopeless, and even cruel, what is happening in the heavenly realm is infused with such wisdom and goodness, with such a plan and a purpose, that if we knew what God was doing we would worship Him and praise Him for whatever is happening around us, no matter how it looks from our human, earthly perspective.

If you're looking for it, this is what you will see again and again throughout the book of Daniel—in fact, throughout the entire Bible.

You'll never watch the news quite the same way again once you start to get a sense of what's going on behind those headlines, what God is doing here on earth to accomplish His eternal, heavenly purposes. For even in times when you have no earthly idea why something occurs, you'll be able to trust that God knows what He's doing—and that His purposes are always good.

COMPREHENSIVE COVERAGE

In the midst of those months I lingered in the book of Daniel, I remember watching the news with my husband one evening. After hearing a rehash of the same three or four storylines that had been dominating the coverage all week, with various guests loudly debating and pontificating about what it all meant, I turned to Robert and exclaimed, "Honey, the book of Daniel is way better than this! It's more timely. It's more helpful. It's definitely more encouraging—and actually more accurate."

If "Heaven rules" were nothing more than a comforting way of processing and absorbing the daily news, this quality alone would make it invaluable (to me at least). Think back again to some of what has bombarded us through our televisions and electronic devices since 2020: the daily graph of new COVID infections and deaths; a contentious, disputed presidential election; racial strife and outrage; rioting and looting; skyrocketing crime rates in American cities and abroad; arguments over masks and vaccines; travel restrictions; businesses shutting down; nursing home residents and hospital patients isolated from their families; churches unable to meet; political battles over immigration and border control; Afghans risking their lives to board moving airplanes to escape conditions in their country; runaway inflation; spiraling gas prices; round-the-clock images of horrific carnage and devastation in Ukraine.

All of this has been real. All of it has actually happened. (And no doubt more is happening as you read this book.) Tuning it out doesn't make it go away. But this relentless deluge of disasters has exacted an emotional toll that most weren't prepared for and left us with questions we're not sure how to answer. Are we simply at the mercy of the next shoe drop? With all the conflicting commentary, who are we to believe? How are we to we handle yet another upsetting breaking news alert? And how are we to deal with the pandemic of depression, despair, loneliness, disorientation, fear, and addiction that has gripped so many of our friends and family members (and perhaps even our own hearts)?

This is where it makes all the difference in the world to orient and tether our hearts to the truth that Heaven rules . . . to affirm by faith what we cannot always see: that Heaven rules over everything, even over those things that threaten the world's peace and well-being. Over economies in crisis. Over contagious new variants. Over powerful tornadoes in the Midwest. Over deadly atrocities in Eastern Europe. God is sovereign over leaders, over nations, over the weather, over all the geopolitical affairs of our world.

Heaven rules over everything, everywhere.

That's what we see in the opening verses of Daniel 1. From earth's perspective, King Nebuchadnezzar took the city of Jerusalem and the nation of Judah captive. But from heaven's vantage point, the king of Babylon was not the ultimate cause behind the city's fall. *God* handed it over to him. Nebuchadnezzar was merely the human instrument God chose to accomplish His purpose.

And as God often does, He had more than one purpose in mind for introducing this set of circumstances into the news cycle. We know, for example, that God wanted to make Himself known to Nebuchadnezzar—as he did later through the king's dream about the mighty tree being cut down (Dan. 4). The Lord had business to transact with this ruler of Babylon. God giving His people into Nebuchadnezzar's hands put Daniel and three of his friends in the king's presence, creating an opportunity for God to speak directly and convincingly to this secular monarch. The fall of Jerusalem—an unmitigated tragedy from the perspective of the Jews forced into exile—set the stage for such encounters to take place.

God's actions in this circumstance also served another purpose. (Who knows how many others there were?) In uprooting His people from their homeland, God was disciplining them for their sin and idolatry, for claiming He was their God when in fact they had forsaken Him as a nation. (The parallels to modern America are all too evident.) As you and I well know, sin in any of its forms, especially idolatry, never ends well for any of us. Sin enslaves us. Sin diminishes us. Sin poisons us and all of our relationships. It ends up doing nothing but hurting us. Why then would God, who sovereignly rules over us and moves providentially toward us, not take the steps needed to bring us to repentance and free us from sin's bondage?

The Bible says that not only did the Lord "hand over" the land of Judah and its king, Jehoiakim, to the Babylonian invaders; He also handed over "some of the vessels from the house of God" into the enemy's possession (Dan. 1:2). This plunder of the temple at the hand of Nebuchadnezzar was a fitting symbol of what had already taken place in the hearts of God's people. Despite years of patient warnings and impassioned appeals from a parade of prophets urging them to repent and return to their God, who was waiting to receive them with mercy and blessing, they had repeatedly refused. So now they had to face God's severe but loving discipline.

MACRO AND MICRO

And once again, God was the One doing all this. *Heaven rules over everything.* Think of this truth as the *macro* perspective—the big picture, like what we'd see through a wide-angle lens or a telescope. This should give us courage and comfort in the midst of the upheaval in our world.

But it's equally comforting and encouraging to realize that *Heaven also rules over the details of our individual lives.* This is the *micro* perspective—the view through a zoom lens or even a microscope. Yes, God rules over the huge events playing out on the national and world stages. But He also rules in the minutiae of our personal lives, events that would never make the evening news.

Daniel 1 provides us a living canvas for observing this personal aspect of God's care and control—the micro view. We're told that in taking Judah captive, Nebuchadnezzar gave orders to "bring some of the Israelites from the royal family and from the nobility—young men without any physical defect, good-looking, suitable for instruction in all wisdom, knowledgeable, perceptive, and capable of serving in the king's palace" (1:3–4). His plan was to set these young men on an intensive three-year training program, a kind of MBA in all things Babylon. While they were training, he would supply them with everything needed for their daily provision, including the best possible food and drink.

It was a classic manipulative ploy, playing on the minds and appetites of the heady, young, and ambitious. King Nebuchadnezzar would show an interest in these elite young men from the aristocratic class, offering them a promising career path in Babylon while progressively breaking down their loyalties to home and family and culture and religious heritage. By plying them with fine wine, royal perks, and the privileges of an imagined inner circle, he could conscript their talents for his own purposes while making them feel both obligated and honored to serve the king who had lavished such honors on them.

We're seeing here a king at his crafty and swaggering best, a king who appears in absolute control, a king who believes he's got this group of young Israelites right where he wants them, with no real choice but to do what he says.

But no. When "invited" (read, *coerced*) into the palace of the known world's greatest power, Daniel still knew who was the true Ruler of the world, the One to whom he answered and to whom he owed his ultimate allegiance. As a result, despite the flak he knew his resistance would generate, Daniel "determined that he would not defile himself with the king's food or with the wine he drank" (Dan. 1:8).[4]

Notice he didn't throw a fit about it. (When you believe that

Heaven rules, you don't have to throw fits in the face of earthly obstacles.) Instead he went directly—and respectfully—to the "chief eunuch" (the person in charge), and "asked permission" not to follow the prescribed diet, which went against the time-honored practice of his faith (1:8).

Note carefully what the Bible says next:

> God had granted Daniel kindness and compassion from the chief eunuch. (1:9)

You might want to write another little "HR" next to that verse. Another "God sighting."

Now tell me who gave Daniel favor with this supervisor. *God did.* Even here in this quote-unquote "advancement program," which everyone in leadership knew was intended to reprogram these backwater Hebrews and instill progressive Babylonian thought in them, God intervened on Daniel's behalf and moved the hearts of his pagan handlers.

So when Daniel appealed to the "guard" (1:11) who was directly responsible for the Hebrew recruits and suggested a ten-day dietary experiment of vegetables and water for him and his three friends, the man agreed to it. Why? Because God had gone before them. Paving the way for them. Protecting them. Providing for them.

"A king's heart is like channeled water in the Lord's hand," the Bible says (Prov. 21:1), as are the hearts of all those in authority, even if they don't acknowledge God. Even if they hate and resist God. Even if they worship other gods, our God still "directs" their hearts "wherever he chooses." There's not a king or leader or president, not even your boss at work, whose heart God cannot touch and turn; not a person God cannot cause to carry out His will.

Because Heaven rules.

But as if favor with a godless administration isn't evidence enough of God's overseeing presence in the lives of Daniel and his friends, the Bible says He also "gave these four young men knowledge and understanding in every kind of literature and wisdom" (Dan. 1:17).

Who gave it? God gave it.

He knew they soon would be encountering situations where they would need these abilities, particularly Daniel's unusual wisdom to understand "visions and dreams of every kind" (1:17). And so based on His knowledge, both of their personal concerns (the micro picture) and of everything else He was orchestrating in the world (the macro picture), God made provision for them, giving them everything they needed just as they needed it and even ahead of when they needed it.

> There's not a king or leader or president, not even your boss at work, whose heart God cannot touch and turn; not a person God cannot cause to carry out His will. Because Heaven rules.

Now these four young men—Daniel, Hananiah, Mishael, and Azariah—certainly weren't the only ones involved in the Babylonian training program for elite young Hebrews. They're just the only four the Bible tells us about. But what we learn from what we're told is that God was mindful of them as individuals and was equipping them with exactly what they required—which wasn't the king's expensive food and wine!—even amid the suffering they were experiencing as victims of a national catastrophe. The same God who rules over nations and who handed Judah over to the king of Babylon (the macro) was also at work in the details of His people's lives (the micro).

And the same is true for you. God will always give you what you need in ways that may not be clear or even visible to you in the moment. But He is preparing you for opportunities and circumstances that lie ahead of you, challenges that may be harder than the ones you're currently experiencing, things you probably don't see coming and may not be able to imagine.

God and God alone knows exactly what's going to happen in your health, in your family, in your finances, in your job, in your country, in this world. All of it.

He's the One who knows. The One who rules. The One who cares. So His work in you, though it may defy conventional logic and may even be painful, if not confusing in the process, is indeed a providing work, a protective work, and a preparatory work. He is putting you in position to display His glory.

Your job and mine is simply to trust Him. And because of who He is, we *can* trust Him. No matter what the situation, we are covered by His watchful love and care and can be assured that He knows the best way to walk us through it. Even when what we are walking through feels unfair as well as painful.

WHY ME?

Daniel and his friends clearly had not forsaken their God or pursued idolatrous lifestyles. And yet they were dealing with the same sense of loss, separation, and displacement as the people whom God was more directly disciplining for their disobedience. The four teenagers could've thought they had every reason to misunderstand God's actions or resent where He had placed them. The whole situation must have felt massively unjust.

You may feel that way, too, at times. Your life may have been made many times more difficult by the choices and sins of others. To borrow the words of Jesus, rain falls on both "the righteous and the unrighteous" (Matt. 5:45). Yet in every tempest and trial, God will move heaven and earth to do whatever is necessary to protect and provide for His children. He will not forget you in the swirl of what's happening around you.

These kinds of settings, in fact, the ones in which the "why me?" questions are easy to ask, are purposeful. In and through all the unknowns, God is carrying out His good, eternal plan. And He often uses these distresses, these injustices, to create a platform from which your life can give powerful witness to His greatness.

Watch and see:

> At the end of the time that the king had said to
> present them, the chief eunuch presented them to
> Nebuchadnezzar. The king interviewed them, and
> among all of them, no one was found equal to Daniel,

Hananiah, Mishael, and Azariah. . . . In every matter of wisdom and understanding that the king consulted them about, he found them ten times better than all the magicians and mediums in his entire kingdom. (Dan. 1:18–20)

> In every tempest and trial, God will move heaven and earth to do whatever is necessary to protect and provide for His children. He will not forget you in the swirl of what's happening around you.

"Ten times better." Advanced in wisdom. Noticeably poised. Strong in character and conviction. Possessing a level of understanding that far surpassed their years.

None of this was what King Nebuchadnezzar expected. None of it was what the chief eunuch or the palace guard expected. It certainly wasn't what the "magicians and mediums" expected, or probably anyone else in the "entire kingdom." None of it squared with earth's perspective on why these four young men had ended up in Babylon.

From earth's perspective these guys were nobodies, prisoners despite their noble birth, not even worth the dignity of being called by their given names. No sooner had they walked in the door than they'd been assigned new Babylonian names. No longer were they to be called Daniel or Mishael (the "el" suffix references *Elohim,* the Hebrew name for the God of Israel, the supreme One, the mighty One). No longer were they to be called Hananiah or Azariah (the "ah" relates to *Yahweh*, the eternal, unchanging, covenant-keeping God).[5] Everything involved in this forced reeducation program of the Hebrews was designed to show them that their old ways were outdated, their old teachers outsmarted, and most of all their old God outmatched by the superior might and stature of Babylon and its gods, including a conquering king named Nebuchadnezzar who thought he was a god.

I'll tell you one thing, though. Nobody names their sons Nebuchadnezzar anymore. But they sure do call a lot of them Daniel.

They do it because there's something special about people who align themselves by faith with what God is doing. There's something different about people who are so convinced God is ruling over the macro world that they can genuinely trust Him to supply and care for them in their micro world. There's something "ten times" more notable about nobodies who only have one answer for what makes them stand out in ways that even the somebodies can't help but notice, desire, and wonder about.

> /\
> Daniel's story inspires us to believe that it is possible for us, too, to remain calm and courageous in the face of crises—both in the way we respond to the macro headlines in the world and the way we deal with the micro headaches and hassles in our personal lives.
> \/

That difference can be seen in a myriad of ways in the lives of those who truly trust Him today:

- when our social media posts are uplifting and God-honoring rather than haranguing about the ineptness of political leaders and the foolishness of their policies
- when we resist the pull of sexual promiscuity and steadfastly choose to practice abstinence until marriage
- when we are faithful to our husband or wife in a world that thinks nothing of looking for satisfaction outside of marriage
- when we refuse to sell our soul to a company by consistently working long hours that require us to neglect our family, even if that means being passed over for promotions and lucrative bonuses
- when we spend years caring for a sick, elderly parent in our home without resentment or complaining
- when we respond to messed-up people and events in this messed-up world with peaceable rather than combative words, forgiveness rather than resentment, mercy rather than vengeance, and humility rather than hubris

Through no fault of his own, Daniel faced an almost unbroken succession of difficulties and troubles throughout his life and career, spanning from his teen years until well into his eighties. His story inspires us to believe that it is possible for us, too, to remain calm and courageous in the face of crises—both in the way we respond to the macro headlines in the world and the way we deal with the micro headaches and hassles in our personal lives.

How?

By lifting up our eyes from earth's perspective to see what is going on from God's perspective. By remembering, as Daniel did, that our confidence is not in the powers that be, but in the all-powerful God of heaven whose we are and whom we serve. By viewing everything that is happening around and to us through the lens of "Heaven rules." And by trusting that, though His ways may not always be easy to discern, our sovereign and providential God is always at work, always carrying out His grand and gracious purposes in all that transpires in this world.

CHAPTER THREE

No Need to Panic

Tears may, and must come;
but if they gather in eyes that are
constantly looking up to You in heaven,
they will glisten with the brightness of the coming glory.

—*Susannah Spurgeon*

LOUIS XIV REIGNED as king of France for a remarkable seventy-two years (1643–1715). He ascended to the throne at the unimaginable age of five, at which time his mother functionally led the country in his stead. But by thirteen he had declared himself in full command, and soon thereafter was parading through the streets of Paris to the resounding shouts of "*Vive le roi!*" ("Long live the king!"). Even at that tender age, the handsome young monarch had already won the hearts of his people.[1]

For his entire reign, Louis lived more or less above the law. He could decide and decree virtually anything he wanted. He was waited on for his every wish. Though some perceived him as a cruel ogre, others considered him a visionary statesman. Whichever the case, he chose as the emblem of his rule the imagery of the sun, proclaiming himself *Roi Soleil,* the Sun King, as if the entire existence of his realm, indeed all of Christendom, orbited around him.

Historians Will and Ariel Durant titled the opening chapter of their eight-hundred-page tome on the life and times of Louis XIV with the following three words: "The Sun Rises." How much more fitting the titling of their closing chapter: "The Sun Sets." [2]

Doesn't it always?

No matter how glorious or inglorious an earthly ruler's season in the spotlight, no matter how long or how brief their tenure, the sun eventually sets on their rule. Whether people love them, fear them, suffer under them, or all of the above, every person who assumes the power of office will at some point reach the end of their time in that office, either by their resignation or retirement, by a loss at the polls, by a successful coup, or, if nothing else, by their death.

But this rhythm of rising and falling is not just a function of age or political opposition or the fickle cry for change from the voting public. Above it all, across all ages of human history, both past and present, stands a God in heaven who "brings down one and exalts another" (Ps. 75:7). Or as Daniel put it,

> He changes the times and seasons;
> he removes kings and establishes kings. (Dan. 2:21)

Earthly rulers only rule because God allows them to rule. And they rule only for as long as He allows them.

The first time I remember seriously pondering this reality

was in a tenth-grade world history class I took at the Christian school I attended. The teacher, a man named Roy Parmelee, was also the varsity boys' basketball coach and was affectionately referred to as Coach Parm. In his class that year we studied the rise and fall of nations throughout history. And while I've long since forgotten much of what we learned about all the kingdoms and empires and conquerors we covered, especially which ones went where and who did what to whom, what I do remember is Coach Parm encouraging us not to think of world events either as merely natural and random occurrences or as completely under human manipulation and control.

> No matter how glorious or inglorious an earthly ruler's season in the spotlight, no matter how long or how brief their tenure, the sun eventually sets on their rule.

At the end of the day, Coach Parm taught us, rulers are not chosen by elections or appointments, by seizures of power, or by any other process, whether man-made or hereditary. God installs them and then removes them whenever He's finished accomplishing what He wants to do with them. We see this dynamic throughout the Bible, and it runs underneath the long march of history. We certainly see it on bright display in the colorful pages of Daniel.

In the truest, ultimate sense, kings (or emperors or presidents or dictators) don't rule. Heaven rules. And any authority wielded by human powers is always and entirely subject to a higher Authority.

Daniel knew this. God gave him the wisdom and insight to recognize it. He seems to have drawn courage from it when, as we saw in the previous chapter, he dared to push back on the dietary plan the king had ordered for new Hebrew subjects in the palace. King Nebuchadnezzar, though he stood so tall, would not be on the throne forever. And his edicts, though handed down with unquestioned authority, remained under the rule of Another.

Despite all its earthly pomp and glory, Nebuchadnezzar's rule was limited by the rising-and-falling arc that the God of heaven maintains over every human enterprise. Daniel used this knowledge as his starting point—the "what" of Heaven's rule, based on the revelation given to him (and to us in Scripture).

But for every "what" there's a "so what"—a "therefore"— the implication and application of the "what." And here's a "so what" that draws my heart to Daniel and to the promise of what we all can experience as we rest in Heaven's rule: Daniel's belief in the unassailable truth that Heaven rules protected him from spiraling into panic even amid tense encounters with the highest-ranking officials of his era, even in situations where his own life was hanging in the balance.

Daniel stayed calm. He didn't waver. In the words of the eighteenth-century Bible commentator Matthew Henry, he was "sedate and even."[3] Cool under pressure. Daniel didn't panic. Daniel *never* panicked.

Was this just a matter of his having a naturally placid

disposition? Or was there something (Someone) he knew that infused him with supernatural confidence?

Clearly the script of Daniel's life, even by his teenage and young adult years, had taken him far from the path he would've chosen if he'd been the one doing the writing. No doubt God's choices regarding kings and nations of the sixth century BC were not easy to understand, even for someone like Daniel who'd been given great understanding. But he knew that God knew what He was doing. And he was convinced that this king, Nebuchadnezzar, under whose earthly regime Daniel now lived, possessed no authority apart from what God had given him. He'd been allowed a measured length of rope for a measured length of time.

So Daniel, despite the dangers and challenges he faced, knew he had nothing to fear. Though he lived and worked in a chaotic world under power-crazy, narcissistic rulers, he was impervious to panic. Not because he was confident in himself, but because no king on earth was stronger than the King in whom Daniel trusted implicitly.

No matter what happened he remained unruffled, because he knew that Heaven rules.

NEITHER STORM NOR FLOOD

To be sure, the "kings" that are exerting their power over you and me today don't exactly resemble King Nebuchadnezzar in Daniel's day. But no doubt there are people and circumstances attempting to control our lives. That's why we must learn to counsel our hearts and minds according to the truth of God's Word: that He is the true, eternal King.

That means cancer is not King.

No pandemic is King.

No demented dictator is King.

Financial concerns and crises are not King.

Injustices committed against us or against those we love are not King.

Other people—a child, a spouse, a parent, a friend, relative, roommate, supervisor, whatever—may have the ability to wound us deeply or even cause our hearts to break. But none of these people is King either. None of them has the power to rule over our emotions, decisions, and reactions.

Only God is King. All others are held in check by Him, rising and falling at His command. And this truth (because it *is* truth) infuses us with spiritual vigor and imparts a sense of equilibrium which we'd have no hope of enjoying otherwise.

During the unforgettable ups and downs (more downs than ups, it seemed) of recent years, in addition to immersing myself in the book of Daniel, I have found myself parked in Psalm 29. Over and over

> ∧
>
> Cancer is not King. No pandemic is King. Financial concerns and crises are not King. Injustices committed against us or against those we love are not King. Only God is King.
>
> ∨

again, through trying days and sometimes wakeful nights, I have meditated on these eleven verses phrase by phrase, reciting and praying them again and again, until they've become a part of the fabric of my being.

The early part of this psalm describes something drastic going on in nature—possibly a massive thunderstorm—symbolizing overwhelming circumstances that threaten to take us under. And the psalm concludes with a resounding statement of faith that affirms God's rule over all of life and creation:

> The LORD sits enthroned over the flood;
> the LORD sits enthroned, King forever.
> The LORD gives his people strength;
> the LORD blesses his people with peace.
> (Ps. 29:10–11)

These two verses, if you will embed them in your heart, will give you enough courage and comfort to last a lifetime, regardless of any floods and storms that may threaten to overwhelm you.

Notice first God's posture (v. 10). What is God doing during these storms? He is sitting. He "sits" above the flood; He "sits" as King forever. He's not nervously pacing the celestial hallways. He's not running around in a panic-stricken frenzy. He's not cobbling together a council to help Him figure out what to do. God is under control. God is *in* control—over and above all things. Nothing is happening in your life or mine, in our nation or anywhere else on the planet, that He is not sovereignly, providentially presiding over.

> ∧
>
> The storms and floods of life happen *beneath* Him, not above Him. This doesn't mean the floods are not dangerous. But it does mean the floods are not final.
>
> ∨

That's the "what." So what's the "so what"?

Here's the "so what": whatever the storm or flood, whether we're feeling ourselves being dragged under by life's problems and pressures or just fearing how much worse they could get, we can still live with "strength" and "peace."

Amazing. How can such seemingly contradictory experiences coexist? Storms and strength? Floods and peace? How can the many varieties of troubles we may face, whether in society at large or in the lives we lead at home or at work, result in something other than debilitating distress and panic?

The answer? Heaven rules. HR. The storms and floods of life happen *beneath* Him, not above Him. Though their waters swell, He is in charge of how far they can reach. And just as surely as He's stirred up those waves, He can also cause them to be still (see Ps. 107:25, 29).

This doesn't mean the floods are not dangerous.

But it does mean the floods are not final.

I've had friends come close to losing their lives in unexpected floods. You and I have watched news coverage of major flooding events, like the one that claimed the lives of 240 people or more in Europe during the summer of 2021. People rightfully get scared in floods. People can drown in floods.

People ride out the night or risk the dangers of seeking higher ground, not knowing how they're going to escape. People can lose their homes and personal possessions in floods. When the waters recede, they're left to pick through the muck and slime of tarnished memories, unable to comprehend how their lives, which seemed to be in such reasonable order just a week before, could now be in such utter ruin and chaos.

Floods are not to be taken lightly.

But watch what your "enthroned" King does and can do—whatever the flood, whatever form it takes in your life. The God who reigns over it reaches down, knowing He has set the boundaries for precisely how long and how wide its waters can rise, and He provides something that marks us as one of His children: "The LORD gives his people strength" (Ps. 29:11).

This statement implies we are weak—and we are. Every one of us faces many circumstances beyond our control in a world that often seems to be falling apart. But "my grace is sufficient for you," the Lord declares to us; "my power is perfected in weakness" (2 Cor. 12:9). That's why we, His people, can humbly, confidently affirm: "When I am weak, then I am strong" (v. 10). Because He who reigns forever over the flood imparts His strength to those who trust Him with their weakness.

He also "blesses his people with peace" (Ps. 29:11). The night before Robert's first cancer surgery, I posted some thoughts on social media:

> Here are three truths we're clinging to as we head into
> surgery tomorrow: (1) Anything that makes us need God

is a blessing. (2) You can trust God to write your story. (3) Heaven rules!

As He has promised, the Lord blessed us with peace that day. And He has been blessing us that way throughout this journey, the peace interrupted only by those times when we forget or fail to believe that Heaven rules.

So if we know this to be true—that God, our one and only King, has made His strength and peace available to us even in situations that feel highly unstable and uncertain—panic is not our only option. Panic, in fact, makes no sense under these conditions. Our God sits enthroned. Our God is "King forever." And He is able to give us not only strength but also peace. So we may have fears, and we may have tears, but we don't have to come undone.

Panic is only for people who don't know that Heaven rules.

Or who don't believe that His rules apply to them.

Let's open our Bibles to Daniel 2, where we'll see an example of a powerful man who desperately needed to learn that *Heaven rules*. This is one of the longest chapters in the book of Daniel. But to get the full impact of this account, I hope you'll take several minutes to read it before we take a look at some of the highlights together.

DREAM SEQUENCE

"In the second year of his reign, Nebuchadnezzar had dreams that troubled him, and sleep deserted him" (Dan. 2:1). And by the time we reach the end of this story, the only person who wouldn't be panicked by the king's bewildering dreams and visions from heaven was Daniel.

Nebuchadnezzar was not the only king in Scripture that God stirred from sleep in order to confront that king's wrongheaded view of life. In Esther 6, for example, God used a ruler's insomnia as part of an orchestrated plan to save the lives of the entire Jewish people. No earthly ruler can hide from the heavenly King, not even in sleep.

Panic is only for people who don't know that Heaven rules. Or who don't believe that His rules apply to them.

Nor can we. But Nebuchadnezzar didn't know that, and the result was almost disastrous.

Part of what unnerved King Nebuchadnezzar, we discover, is that he'd awakened in a cold sweat from these unforgettable nightmares, unable to remember what he'd dreamed about. But the king had a plan for such a contingency. He called on his staff of "magicians, mediums, sorcerers, and Chaldeans" (2:2)—basically practitioners of the occult who claimed supernatural powers of discernment. Part of their job was conjuring up interpretations of any happenings the king observed that he considered to be signs or omens. So, unable to sleep, Nebuchadnezzar summoned these men and said to them, "I have had a dream and am anxious to understand it" (2:3).

"Say no more," they replied in essence—except, of course, he would need to say what he'd dreamed.

But that was the problem. Nebuchadnezzar couldn't remember the dream! Why did they think he'd called them over in the middle of the night in such a panic if he wasn't desperate to recover the contents of this dream before the whole night escaped him entirely? The clock was ticking! Time was of the essence! And all his team of "wise men" could do was stall for more time!

By now Nebuchadnezzar was *really* fuming. In the explosive moments that followed, he alternately threatened his advisors with annihilation ("If you don't tell me the dream and its interpretation, you will be torn limb from limb, and your houses will be made a garbage dump," 2:5) and trying to cut a deal with them ("If you make the dream and its interpretation known to me, you'll receive gifts, a reward, and great honor from me," 2:6).

Remember, this was the most powerful man on the earth, the king of the mighty Babylonian empire, and he was coming completely unglued. Keep that in mind as you read. And compare that picture to that of the King seated "enthroned over the flood," the One who "gives his people strength," the One who "blesses his people with peace."

Finally, the king's panel of pagan experts came as close to voicing a statement of truth as anyone had during this entire nighttime episode: "No one on earth can make known what the king requests" (2:10). Right you are, wise man. This demand the king was making was impossible. "What the king is asking is so difficult," they added, "that no one can make it known to him except the gods, whose dwelling is not with mortals"

(2:11). Not completely true, but in the ballpark.

At this, Nebuchadnezzar's rage became violently irrational. He barked out a blanket decree for the immediate execution not only of the counselors currently in his presence but of "all the wise men of Babylon" (2:12). All of them.

This is where the story bends around to Daniel and his three friends. The four young men were technically among this group of royal advisors, having been assigned to these positions by (so it seemed) the king himself because of how they'd impressed him during his interview with them in Daniel 1. Little did King Nebuchadnezzar realize, when he recognized the talents of these Hebrews he thought he'd conquered all by himself, that he was only doing the bidding of the King of heaven.

But being counted among the people of God does not exempt us from the ordeals of living in a sinful, fallen world or from the rising floods that flow from it in all directions. Things looked bad for Daniel in that moment, as in many moments throughout our own lives as believers. The kings of the earth can appear too strong for us. In many ways they are.

But Daniel had something the other so-called wise men— those who were thrown into panic because of the reach and rashness of Nebuchadnezzar's death sentence—did not possess. When the king's henchman pounded the pavement to Daniel's quarters, then pounded on his door announcing his intentions, Daniel stepped forward with an unexpected response, a response triggered by his awareness that for every event we can see here on earth there is another, truer heavenly perspective.

Daniel responded with tact and discretion to Arioch, the
captain of the king's guard, who had gone out to execute
the wise men of Babylon. (Dan. 2:14)

"With tact and discretion." Not panic.

Daniel calmly inquired, "Why is the decree from the king so
harsh?" (2:15). And Arioch, this officer of the crown, surprised
that a man who only had hours to live was neither running for
his life nor begging to be spared, is described in Scripture as taking time to explain the situation to Daniel in full. Like maybe
over coffee. With perhaps a heartfelt apology for having to carry
out his duty. What a contrast Daniel's demeanor must have
made to the reception this man had encountered at the other
doors he'd visited that day, the doors of those who thought the
king of heaven sat on the throne of Babylon. What Arioch saw
in Daniel was something completely different and unexpected.

Strength, with peace.

Peace, with strength.

This is not just a personality trait, not just a reflection of
Daniel's natural disposition. Daniel exuded the quiet assurance
of someone grounded in an understanding that Heaven rules.
It's the same quiet assurance that you and I, too, can experience
within us and radiate around us whenever we're startled by the
next piece of upsetting news arriving on our doorstep.

Trouble? Turmoil? False accusations? Flood warnings?

No, it's not good. But it's no time for panic.

Heaven rules.

PEACE IN OUR TIME

As our world was churning wildly in 2020, I recorded a short podcast series called *Coronavirus, Cancer, and Christ*. I wanted to counsel my own heart with God's Word as well as encourage others—those who, like Robert and me, felt overwhelmed by the storms and floods that were daily in our inboxes and news feeds, if not directly in our faces. In the process of preparing this new series, I went back through the transcripts of some sessions I'd taught in the past and found that I was preaching to myself! Here are a few excerpts that particularly spoke to me:

> God is good even when you don't feel like He is good. God loves you with a steadfast love even when you feel like He has abandoned you. God is with you in this storm. He will never leave you!

> Remember what God has done in the past. Rely on His character. Rehearse His promises. Refrain from taking matters into your own hands. Don't let fear drive you to places God doesn't want you to go!

> God uses events that turn our world upside down to drive us to cling to Him.

> As we face medical fears and economic fears, we can lean entirely on Christ as our fortress and our strength.

> Wherever trouble is present, God is more present![4]

Two things come to mind as I read through these words again, remembering the types of events, both macro (cultural, political, the pandemic) and micro (Robert's cancer), that were playing out in that season.

First, I'm freshly challenged, as I hope you are, to keep myself grounded in the places where God has kept my heart grounded before. When we're in a crisis, we react based on whatever we've been most accustomed to thinking about and seeing and believing and experiencing. And if we've been in the habit of dwelling on God's truth, if that's what we've been regularly saturating our minds and counseling our hearts with, His truth will settle around our souls in that moment—sheltering us, providing a safe refuge, even as the storm or flood strikes.

Second, stories like Daniel's and others the Lord has preserved for us in Scripture give a more accurate reading on what's actually happening not only in the world back then but also in our world today.

I think, for example, of the apostles Peter and John encountering life-threatening opposition for daring to declare their faith in the risen Christ. They knew that God, though reigning as King, had allowed His Son's determined enemies "to do whatever [God's] hand and . . . will had predestined to take place" by putting Him to death on the cross (Acts 4:28). But having witnessed God turning the most glaring injustice of all time (Christ's crucifixion) into a triumph of His rule (Christ's resurrection), they could pray with confidence concerning the people who now opposed *them,* "Lord, consider their threats, and grant that your servants may speak your word with all boldness" (v. 29). God's actions in the past defined their panic-free courage and trust in Him in the present.

But even beyond these biblical accounts that steady my heart, almost every day, if I'm looking and listening for them, I hear stories of God's strength-giving, peace-giving faithfulness in the lives of people right around me.

Not long ago I sat in a hotel lobby late into the night, catching up with a longtime friend I'd not seen in several years. She has been a faithful lover and servant of Christ since she was a teen. But storms came crashing in around her when she learned that her husband of thirty-some years, who had served in vocational ministry for decades, had been living a lie for a very long time. One wave of painful revelations after another washed over her—a sordid affair, dozens of dalliances with women who were complete strangers, and an endless web of deception to cover it all up.

In the aftermath, she of course has grieved deeply, as much for her husband's soul as for her own loss. And while she grieved, she has been forced to make horrifically difficult decisions and take steps she could not have imagined when she and her husband were happily serving the Lord together. The life she once experienced has changed for the worse in almost every way imaginable and has devastated her children, her finances, and her health.

But as I listened to her story, I was struck that the woman sitting at my side was not emotionally overwrought, nor has she been overcome by her husband's sinful choices. She models a quiet strength and peace because the betrayal and crises brought on by her faithless husband are not "king" in her life. Christ is King. Nor are those life-altering calamities final. Christ is with her in her present pain. And beyond the heartaches of this life, He has promised her a glorious, eternal future that will make all she has suffered become dim in comparison.

We are not doomed to despair, despite the floods of anguish and adversity we may face, despite alarming threats to our health and safety, despite the insistence of those who believe they can act against us in whatever way they choose, and despite the sense that we have no recourse because their behavior seems beyond God's ability or willingness to intervene.

Things that seem immovable on earth are not immovable to the King of heaven. "He changes the times and seasons," Daniel declared when the king's dream was revealed to him in answer to prayer. "He removes kings and establishes kings" (Dan. 2:21).

Sooner or later, this immovable truth will be recognized by every ruler on earth and by all those under their authority.

METAL FRAGMENTS

"Are you able to tell me the dream I had and its interpretation?" the king asked Daniel (2:26). Clearly he was thinking, *How? Because no one else can!*

Daniel, having maintained such composure in questioning the captain about the king's death sentence, apparently had won a stay of execution. After that he'd gone to his friends to appeal for prayer, and now he was in Nebuchadnezzar's presence, ready with the following response to the king's side-eyed question:

> "No wise man, medium, magician, or diviner is able to make known to the king the mystery he asked about. But there is a God in heaven who reveals mysteries." (Dan. 2:27–28)

And this God had important news to share with Nebuchadnezzar, news that only the God over heaven *and* earth could know. It had to do with both the present and the future, with kings rising and kings falling.

Nebuchadnezzar's dream, as Daniel reconstructed it for him, involved a "colossal statue," "tall and dazzling," "terrifying" in appearance (2:31), and composed of various metals and other substances. Its head was made of gold, its shoulders and arms of silver, its torso of bronze, its legs of iron, and its feet a mixture of iron and clay. According to Daniel, these four metals—gold, silver, bronze, and iron, decreasing in value from head to foot—represented four different empires, beginning with Nebuchadnezzar's current Babylonian empire, then continuing on through three others as time marched along.

Okay, and this means what exactly?

At least three "Heaven rules" principles stand out to me from this dream and its meaning as explained by God through Daniel.

HR PRINCIPLE #1: **All human power comes from God.**

The "head of gold" stood for Nebuchadnezzar himself. "The God of the heavens," Daniel said to him, "has given you sovereignty, power, strength, and glory" (2:37). Note where the power came from: "*God . . . has given.*" Never forget that. "Wherever people live—or wild animals, or birds of the sky—*he* has handed them over to you and made you ruler over them all" (2:38).

Imagine a person of Nebuchadnezzar's abilities and influence operating his life around that principle, the idea that nothing he possessed was earned, that he owed everything pertaining to his prominent position to the "God of the heavens." His whole future might have been different. His season of insanity might have been avoided. His kingdom and his people might have been set up for generation after generation of blessing.

The opportunity to lead does not begin with us. Power and leadership are gifts from God.

HR PRINCIPLE #2: **No earthly ruler or kingdom will last forever.**

"After you, there will arise another kingdom" (2:39). Be sure to remember this verse too. Of every president, prime minister, king, or any other earthly ruler, it can invariably be said, "After you, there will arise another kingdom."

King Louis XIV, for all his seventy-some-odd years of ruling, eventually saw the sun go down on his reign, and his crown went to his grandson, Louis XV. Nebuchadnezzar, we know, ruled for more than forty years, during which time it was easy for a man of his pride and self-importance to believe he might just go on being king forever. But that just wasn't true. Nor is it true in regard to any "ruler" in any sphere of life, whether in government, at work, at church, or in any other context. God raises up leaders in specific times and places, for His eternal purposes. But no human will reign forever.

Reaching beyond Nebuchadnezzar and his times, the remainder of the statue imagery spoke prophetically about the centuries to come. The increasingly inferior metals were the visual equivalents of then-future empires, each one less powerful and progressively more vulnerable than the Babylonian Empire. Babylon would eventually be conquered and displaced by the Medo-Persians (the silver), who would fall to the Greeks (the bronze), who would fall to the Romans (the iron). In time the far-flung groups of people the Romans formed into an empire would prove incapable of holding together (the iron mixed with clay). We can verify now from established history that all of these things happened just as God predicted they would, just as He made known to Daniel to tell Nebuchadnezzar.

But that's not all. The king's dream contained a final, dramatic component, which is probably what frightened him the most in his sleep. Daniel recounted it this way:

> "As you were watching, a stone broke off without a hand touching it, struck the statue on its feet of iron and fired clay, and crushed them. Then the iron, the fired clay, the bronze, the silver, and the gold were shattered and

became like chaff from the summer threshing floors. The wind carried them away, and not a trace of them could be found." (2:34–35)

This part of the king's dream is not hard to understand. Here we see graphically depicted the certain future of all human systems, rule, and pride—all those powerful earthly kingdoms crushed, shattered, their dust blown away by the wind, until there is nothing left of them.

And what then?

HR PRINCIPLE #3: The kingdom of God will overcome and outlast all earthly kingdoms.

"But the stone that struck the statue became a great mountain and filled the whole earth" (2:35). The Rock that pulverizes these kings and kingdoms is raised up until it towers over and pervades every part and particle of the earth.

> "In the days of those kings, the God of the heavens will set up a kingdom that will never be destroyed, and this kingdom will not be left to another people. It will crush all these kingdoms and bring them to an end, but will itself endure forever." (2:44)

No matter how imposing or impressive any earthly nation or its rulers appear—no matter how certain of its standing or how devoted to its destiny—it contains a crushing in its future.

Think of the "so what" to that statement. We can (and should) be patriotic toward the country we call home, and we can (and should) ask God to give us leaders who rule with wisdom and justice. But there's a faulty grid in place if we ever place our hope in the "kingdom" of any particular nation or political party or candidate. The only kingdom that will matter eternally is the kingdom of God. Let us fly no other flag so high or make any pledge so passionately as the one that goes,

> "Your kingdom come.
> Your will be done
> on earth as it is in heaven." (Matt. 6:10)

Because the statue of all human kingdoms will someday fall, by His hand and at His feet.

And everyone, I believe, at least at some point in their life, instinctively suspects it. Even a king like Nebuchadnezzar had a moment of being floored by it. When Daniel had finished his retelling of the king's dream and its interpretation, "Nebuchadnezzar fell facedown" (Dan. 2:46). In the only way he knew, he worshiped Daniel's God, offering praise and gifts, and saying, "Your God is indeed God of gods, Lord of kings, and a

> ∧
>
> Let us fly no other flag so high or make any pledge so passionately as the one that goes, "Your kingdom come. Your will be done on earth as it is in heaven" (Matt. 6:10).
>
> ∨

revealer of mysteries" (2:47). This king of Babylon had a feeling, be it ever so fleeting, that the crown he wore on earth belonged to the King who rules from heaven.

How much more should *we* know it—and live like it. Because if we did, it would change a lot about how worked up we become when the news gets bad—on the macro level: when the numbers are reported, when the cities rage, when the future seems bleak. And on the micro level: when our bills are mounting, when people we love keep failing us. When we keep failing ourselves.

Hope *never* fails when we truly believe that Heaven rules.

The dream that God gave to King Nebuchadnezzar and revealed to Daniel—it's not a dream. It's real. It is happening. The "stone" that shattered the kingdoms that made up the statue is the Rock of ages who will come in God's time and in God's way to smash all the kingdoms of the earth and bring judgment on all who've rejected Him. The vision given to the apostle John in the book of Revelation describes it this way, in one of my favorite passages in all of Scripture:

> I saw heaven opened, and there was a white horse. Its
> rider is called Faithful and True, and with justice he
> judges and makes war. His eyes were like a fiery flame,
> and many crowns were on his head. He had a name
> written that no one knows except himself. He wore a
> robe dipped in blood, and his name is called the Word
> of God. The armies that were in heaven followed him

on white horses, wearing pure white linen. A sharp sword came from his mouth, so that he might strike the nations with it. He will rule them with an iron rod. He will also trample the winepress of the fierce anger of God, the Almighty. And he has a name written on his robe and on his thigh: KING OF KINGS AND LORD OF LORDS. (Rev. 19:11–16)

Hallelujah. This day is coming. The King is coming. He's coming to judge the kingdoms of this earth and to establish His kingdom in this world—a kingdom that can never be destroyed. We have His promise. And if we're looking through eyes of faith, we can already see glimpses of that day.

The most corrupt, the most incompetent, rulers of this age are only cause for alarm if we view them merely from earth's perspective. Because from heaven's perspective, from eternity's vantage point, they're no cause for us to panic at all.

And we could all do with a lot less panicking.

TEACHABLE MOMENTS

I think back to that tenth-grade classroom where day after day Coach Parm told us about the risings and fallings of different kings, kingdoms, and nations, reminding his students that we weren't just learning names and dates. We were watching the rule of God at work across time, right here on the earth.

And in God's providence, the lessons I was learning in the

classroom that year were vividly reinforced for me in the labo-
ratory of life.

The night before school started that September of my soph-
omore year—which made me roughly the age of Daniel when
his young life in Judah began falling apart—my family's house
was badly damaged in a fire. All of us were spared, thank God.
But I, along with my six younger brothers and sisters, had to be
farmed out to other families in the area while my parents worked
to get us moved into a new home. That's how my school year
began, with the four walls of familiarity and security crumbling
around me.

Over the course of that same year, my dad's business went
through a period of steep decline. Despite years of his initia-
tive, hard work, and leadership, the company, which had grown
into a great success, suddenly came under rigorous attack. A
once-thriving business now suffered huge losses.

Then, right around the close of that school year, my mother
was diagnosed with a life-threatening brain tumor. Another
shocker. As if the beginning and middle of the year hadn't
brought enough struggle, it ended not with subsiding pressures and a return to normalcy, but with a new, worse threat.
She would require serious brain surgery, and the outcome was
unknown.[5] The flood waters that had been rising now threatened to engulf my entire world.

I sat in a classroom each weekday of that year with my world
history book open, studying the history of nations and powers
while trying to process one traumatic personal loss after another.

But in the classroom of life God had me enrolled in, as I listened to His wisdom through teachers, parents, pastors, and His Word, I learned that God was not there to guarantee we would always have prosperity and success, nor was He mistreating us by taking us through the thrashing waves. I learned that comfort and courage, strength and peace, come from a God who rules over all the risings and fallings in our lives, just as He rules over the risings and fallings in every other place, in every time, around the globe.

During that significant year, what I had previously known theologically proved to be precious, rock-solid truth that could and would preserve my heart in every crisis.

Our God is King. He rules over every flood and storm.

So be still, my soul. There's no need to panic.

CHAPTER FOUR

Can I Get a Witness?

God makes himself look glorious
whenever I trust him with my disappointments.
Far from tarnishing his good name,
my smile in my wheelchair
turns up the wattage on his glory for others to see.

—*Joni Eareckson Tada*

IF YOU KNOW THE STUNNED feeling of being told you have cancer, you also know the conflicting thoughts and emotions that can whipsaw within your heart in the weeks and months that follow. The shock and questions. The fear and determination. The dread of what the future grind entails, and yet the impatience to get it started.

My longtime friend Debby Canfield knows all of those feelings. For almost fifty years she has served alongside her husband, Steve, in the ministry I have been a part of for most of those years. She is a mother of six and grandmother of nineteen (so far), as well as being a speaker and mentor of women. In the spring of 2021, Debby received the disturbing news that a lump in her breast was indeed cancerous. Options and timelines were discussed. In short order she and her team of medical advisors had agreed on a treatment plan. She was scheduled for a mastectomy in six weeks.

Debby and Steve arrived at the hospital early on that Wednesday morning and checked in. Debby was quickly taken back to the pre-op area. By midmorning she was prepped and waiting for the eleven o'clock procedure. Waiting. Waiting. Finally, around noon, a nurse stepped in to inform her that the doctor was still in surgery. They could still work Debby in, not to worry, but it would need to be later in the afternoon.

More waiting. Apprehension mounted as an hour's delay turned into a few hours, then into five or six. Steve and Debby calculated that by the time Debby's surgery would start, the surgeon would already have been in the operating room for ten hours. Plus, with the current COVID restrictions in place, Steve wouldn't be allowed to remain waiting with her, and she'd be left in the hospital all alone.

After praying together they decided to reschedule the surgery, only to find out that the soonest they could get the procedure done was two weeks later.

What a mess. *Why, Lord?*

But Heaven rules. Steve and Debby think that way. (Would that all of us thought that way.) A night or two later, instead of continuing to stew about it, they asked another couple in our ministry, John and Donna Avant, if they'd like to go out to eat, maybe come to the house afterward and play a game.

By early evening the four of them were seated together at a local restaurant, ordering dinner. Their server, a young woman I'll call Stacy, had already been over to make her tableside introductions. She explained—in case it showed—that she had only been working there two or three days and was still learning on the fly. She was also new to the area and working two jobs to get her feet under her.

When she came back to take their orders, Steve noticed a portion of 1 Corinthians 13 tattooed on Stacy's forearm. He asked her about it. "Oh," she said, "those are my mom's favorite verses."

"So you're a Christian?"

"Well, no, I'm not really sure. My mom prays for me all the time, but . . . I just don't know if God's real, you know? But hey, I'm open to a sign that she's right, that maybe He really is there."

Hmm.

Recognizing a gospel opportunity, Steve and Debby's friend John spoke up: "How's this for a sign, Stacy? The Lord just sent four missionaries to your table on your third day of work."

Whoa! Her eyes widened. Her face flushed. She was listening. Throughout the entire meal, as she crisscrossed back and forth to their table, they continued to share with her, and she continued wanting to hear more.

John finally said, "Stacy, would you like to receive Christ? Would you like to know the love those verses on your arm talk about?"

In less than a minute she was back. "Yes! Yes, I would."

Quickly but gently Steve walked Stacy through the gospel,

being careful to remind her how serious a commitment she'd be making—a lifelong promise, one requiring repentance and faith, but one that would change her life forever, just as Christ had changed theirs. John then led her in prayer—an answer to her mother's prayers—right there around the dishes and tea glasses.

As these four friends were driving away together, still beaming from the joy of their shared experience that night, Donna turned to Debby and said, "You know, if you'd had that surgery on Wednesday when it was planned, we wouldn't have gone to dinner tonight, we wouldn't have met Stacy, and we couldn't have told her about Jesus."

True, isn't it? She's so right.

Their testimony to Stacy that night was also a testament to Heaven's rule.

Apply Debby's situation to your own life for a moment. She'd felt so discouraged during that long, disappointing day at the hospital. Rescheduling her surgery only prolonged the start of her cancer fight. It meant undoing and remaking all the plans she'd put in place for her recovery period. It delayed her sense of making progress and triggered niggling worries that the disease could progress in the few weeks.

But what was heaven's perspective on this turn of events she couldn't control? And what might be heaven's perspective on yours? What difference does this HR principle make when something happens that doesn't agree with your agenda, when the situation in question just doesn't make any sense to you and doesn't seem to be taking your feelings into account?

- Your car not starting meant getting a ride—maybe even a tow—having to explain why you were late, and then needing to make another inconvenient trip to the repair shop. You really don't have time for this, especially right now, with everything else you've got going on, but . . . Heaven rules.

- You were nervous about accepting that ministry position at church. You would never have said yes when you were asked if you'd known how much time your parents' health needs were going to demand. You're worried you're going to fail at all of it. But . . . Heaven rules.

- You've come to dread the holidays, at least the get-togethers with extended family now that the family dysfunction has become too obvious and uncomfortable to ignore. There's a part of you that doesn't even want to be with those people anymore. But you go anyway. You set aside your desires for a stress-free break, because . . .

You know the answer. Because you believe Heaven rules. Even if what's happened conflicts with your plans. Even if it stretches you beyond your limit. Even if it forces you outside your comfort zone and into a conversation that puts you on the spot. It might just set the stage for God to show up.

And to make your life a testimony.

PARTAKE OF THE INTERRUPTION

"Your God," Nebuchadnezzar said to Daniel, after the king's dream had been revealed and interpreted to him—"is indeed God of gods, Lord of kings" (Dan. 2:47). I can't think of anything I'd rather hear said to me by an unbeliever.

- "Nancy, your God is amazing."
- "Your God truly answers prayer."
- "Your God must really be God."

I want my witness for Christ to be such that those who don't know Him would be compelled to say, "I want your God to be my God." Wouldn't you love that yourself? We want our lives to be a winsome, walking testimony of His goodness and greatness.

You know what? Believing and living as if Heaven rules can take care of that for us.

Daniel, you recall, was just sitting at home, minding his own business, when the whole "kill every member of my counseling department" directive went out and he found himself swept up in unwanted drama. Being unjustly incriminated was obviously not how he'd planned on spending the day, any more than he'd planned on facing the king with news that could have sent the high-strung tyrant into an even angrier tirade.

And yet the intrusion didn't send Daniel reeling or cause him to implode emotionally. Why? Because he believed that Heaven rules. He viewed God as being in control of every circumstance, and no injustice or personal threat could lessen Daniel's resolve to honor Him. As a result, the morning that had started so badly ended with the pagan king of Babylon praising the God Daniel worshiped.

You see, these unwelcome interruptions, detours, and trials are often God's ticket to our testimony. They provide a platform for us to make much of our Father in the eyes of a watching world—or simply in the eyes of one other person who desperately needs to know that He is real and He is good.

You and I will never lack for opportunities to share and live out our witness, demonstrating what's different about a person who follows our God, and making His reality difficult for others to refute. The Lord will make sure of this, simply in the flow of His rule in your life. And if you'll start each day already certain that you'll give Him your worship when those difficult moments come, no matter how you're challenged or how you feel, your testimony to your God will speak volumes. That can begin for you today.

To further prove the point, I call as my next witness . . . well, three witnesses:

Their names are Shadrach, Meshach, and Abednego. Chances are that Daniel 3—the story of Daniel's three friends in the fiery furnace—is already quite familiar to you. But I hope you'll take a moment to read this chapter anyway to refresh your memory. If it's new to you, by all means read it to acquaint yourself with this dramatic account. How did the trial faced by these young men became an opportunity to shine a spotlight on Heaven's rule?

A TALE OF THREE WITNESSES

These three friends of Daniel had, at his request, been appointed by Nebuchadnezzar to administrative posts in the Babylonian government. These positions came as a result of the favor God continued to give Daniel following the events surrounding the king's mysterious dream. That's why later, when the palace "sent word to assemble the satraps, prefects, governors, advisers, treasurers, judges, magistrates, and all the rulers of the provinces to attend the dedication of the statue King Nebuchadnezzar had set up" (Dan. 3:2), there was no getting out of it. Attendance was mandatory.

Yet so was their belief that no matter what kind of turn this day took, they would trust God with the outcome, no questions asked. They would be respectful as citizens of this nation, and they would perform their duties to this king and this people. But their supreme allegiance, as always, would be to God as His servants, committed to doing His will in all places, at all costs.

This statue that formed the focal point of the day's festivities brings to mind another statue—the one the king had seen in his earlier nightmare. God had used that visual in Daniel 2 to explain to Nebuchadnezzar that his power to reign came from God alone and that God would bring his kingdom to an end. But then Nebuchadnezzar turned around and constructed a colossal statue in honor of . . . himself.

Seems he had entirely missed the point of the dream.

The irony is almost grotesque, as was the statue itself—ninety feet tall, roughly the height of an eight-story building, and nine feet wide. And whereas the statue in the dream had represented Nebuchadnezzar as the "head of gold," this statue was *all* gold. Probably not solid gold, since it couldn't have been raised upright at that weight, but perhaps a wooden structure of some kind covered in gold.[1] But no doubt this massive object made the desired impression by the way it gleamed in the sunlight, towering over the assembled dignitaries.

You can imagine the discomfort of Shadrach, Meshach, and Abednego at the idolatry they were witnessing, the very sin that had proven so costly to their own people. But discomfort became a shiver when the call came ringing out, blared loudly by the voice of an on-site herald:

> "People of every nation and language, you are
> commanded: When you hear the sound of the horn,
> flute, zither, lyre, harp, drum, and every kind of music,
> you are to fall facedown and worship [mark that word
> *worship*] the gold statue that King Nebuchadnezzar has
> set up." (3:4–5)

And lest anyone should think they were exempt from the king's maniacal order:

> "Whoever does not fall down and worship will
> immediately be thrown into a furnace of blazing fire."
> (3:6)

Shadrach, Meshach, and Abednego's day had just gone from bad to worse.

Or in the realm of "Heaven rules," from ordinary to testimony.

THE WAR FOR WORSHIP

Let's not kid ourselves into feeling twenty-six centuries removed from their dilemma. This battle for worship is not only as old as the garden of Eden; it's as fresh as this morning's coffee. The world around us is constantly tugging on us, teasing us, sometimes taunting us to give our worship to created things and beings, worship that belongs only to God our Creator. The list of "statues" we're pressured to worship is long and sadly familiar. Celebrity. Success. Work. Wealth. Fans and popularity. Other people's possessions and achievements. Government as our provider and political leaders as saviors. Comfort. Cultural conformity, at whatever cost to our conscience and what we claim to be our convictions.

And don't expect it to let up. This battle will be among us for as long as the earth endures, until eventually, as Revelation 13 tells us, believers will face intense pressure to bow the knee to what's described as the "image of the beast" (Rev. 13:14). Once again, in haunting similarity to the dynamic of Daniel 3, whoever does not "worship" the enemy's likeness in that day will be killed (v. 15).

We're already feeling this pressure today—in some parts of the world more than others. Ask believers in Nigeria, in parts of

India, in China. The persecution faced by literally millions today in countries and people groups around the globe is real, though it may be far away and hidden from our view.[2] But even for those of us who have enjoyed the blessing of religious liberty, this battle for worship may one day escalate to life-or-death proportions, as it did in Nebuchadnezzar's Babylon for three children of God.

Whenever and wherever we face that battle in the future, will our knees buckle in fear of the consequences, or will we take our stand on the truth that Heaven rules?

What kind of testimony do we have now and will we have then before the powers and rulers of this world?

You probably know the story of what happened when Shadrach, Meshach, and Abednego remained on their feet while everyone else bowed and worshiped. A group of local officials, perhaps jealous of these Jews who had been promoted above them to positions of importance, rushed to get the king's attention, making sure he hadn't failed to notice the disregard for his "deity" that these three men—*Those three, over there!*—were displaying by standing tall before the massive statue while all others had fallen to their knees.

Nebuchadnezzar, true to type, became irate. "In a furious rage" (Dan. 3:13), he ordered the three men brought before him, where he repeated the edict to "fall down and worship the statue I made" or else face the fires of his royal furnace. "And who," he thundered, "is the god who can rescue you from my power?" (3:15).

But like Daniel before them, these three men did not panic.

They showed no sense of terror. I love that. I want that. This day had not caught them by surprise, because it never does when we recognize that Heaven rules. Nor could the king's terrifying threats move them to worship his imposing statue, because they'd already determined that their worship belonged wholly and only to heaven's Ruler.

There's testimony in that. Just in that. There's even more in how Shadrach, Meshach, and Abednego responded to the question the king—a self-proclaimed god—had posed about their own God.

> "Nebuchadnezzar, we don't need to give you an answer
> to this question. If the God we serve exists, then he can
> rescue us from the furnace of blazing fire, and he can
> rescue us from the power of you, the king. But even if he
> does not rescue us, we want you as king to know that we
> will not serve your gods or worship the gold statue you
> set up." (3:16–18)

Do you wonder, as I have, if you could take the same stand these three men did, with all that pressure to compromise, with their lives in the balance? I feel sure they'd had their moments of wondering too. But as you ponder what it will be like one day—which is increasingly feeling like today—when believers will be made to choose between worshiping the "image of the beast" or accepting their deaths, will you be able to do it? Will I? We wonder.

And yet, as with Shadrach, Meshach, and Abednego, the Lord

even now is in the process of preparing us. In their case, before facing this larger test, He'd already been giving them smaller tests, such in the matter of refusing the king's food in favor of what their God prescribed. And they'd been passing these tests and learning from them little by little, all along the way.

The same is true for you and me. All these opportunities God gives us—the little challenges, the little interruptions, the everyday moments when we must choose to obey or to compromise, to complain or accept, to give Him grief or give Him honor—they're building something in us. They're strengthening the resolve of our relationship with Him. They're solidifying the reality in our hearts that Heaven rules—in all places, at all times. So when we face an even harder test, our hearts will be prepared to give testimony even there.

"All things work together," right? All His plans are working out His plan for us, "for the good of those who love God," for the good of those "who are called according to his purpose" (Rom. 8:28). His rule in our hearts, resulting in our testimony.

That's why in Revelation we read of our brothers and sisters in Christ who overcame the power of the enemy—how?

> By the blood of the Lamb
> and by the word of their testimony;
> for they did not love their lives
> to the point of death. (Rev. 12:11)

Are these believers somehow different from you? Or me? No. Count yourself among them if you've believed on Christ for your salvation. And "rejoice" (v. 12)—yes, *rejoice!*—that He is daily equipping you through this HR boot camp of life to be an ongoing, overcoming witness to your God. Through it all. All the way home.

What a testimony He is preparing you to deliver.

JESUS IN THE FIRE

One Friday night in late 2021, the red curtain went up on Nashville's Grand Ole Opry stage. Every weekend for ninety years, the superstars and wannabes of country music have entertained on that stage with their rollicking songs of love and loss, of good times and the good Lord.

But that night was a little different. A piano player no one had ever heard drew a rousing standing ovation for his rendition of a beloved gospel song.[3]

Only one week earlier, on the previous Friday night, a historic line of tornadoes had torn through four states in the American South. The twisters had remained on the ground, chewing up houses and property, along a continuous path of two hundred miles. The devastation was horrific, the loss of life utterly heartbreaking.

In the days that followed, among countless reports of tragedy as well as touching stories of neighbors helping neighbors, a video emerged that quickly went viral.[4] It shows a Kentucky dad, his back to the camera beneath the roofless remains of his debris-littered home. Against one wall, now open to the sun beaming down where the ceiling used to be, Jordan Baize sits on a wooden piano bench playing the tinny, waterlogged notes of Bill and Gloria Gaither's classic praise song, "There's Something about That Name."

The phone camera pans the scene: exposed rafters, ruptured door jambs, the shattered picture frames, the fallen Christmas tree. And yet lilting above it, as if untouched by the visible evidence of what lies before him, wafts this musical refusal to bow in defeat before losses that feel permanent but are limited in what they can take. That day, and on Jordan's Opry appearance a week later,[5] Heaven's rule was declared before a spellbound world.

> There's nothing sugary about a "Heaven rules" witness. You won't hear me comparing the bold, confident confession of Heaven's rule to a fairy-tale ending—at least not yet. We never know what we're stepping into when we choose worship of God over what comes more naturally to us.

Testimony. To the things "our God" can do when HR is our answer to everything.

Notice, though, that the testimony often grows out of real pain and suffering. There's nothing sugary about a "Heaven rules" witness. You won't hear me comparing the bold, confident confession of Heaven's rule to a fairy-tale ending—at least not yet. We never know what we're stepping into when we choose worship of God over what comes more naturally to us—the fear of man and the tendency to prostrate ourselves before earthly powers, trends, and demands. When we give our witness, we may face ridicule, anger, dismissiveness, or worse. We may be talked about, lied about, taken advantage of, and considered crazy.

The three men in ancient Babylon were well aware that their unwavering allegiance to their God would be costly. They knew full well that they might be required to pay the ultimate price of their lives. And that's exactly what happened—almost, at least.

King Nebuchadnezzar, erupting again in rage at Shadrach, Meshach, and Abednego's devotion and defiance, ordered the furnace stoked to seven times its normal output, leaving no doubt about what those flames would do to them. Not even the soldiers who'd been ordered to tie them up and throw them into the fire survived the mission. Between their urgency to carry out the king's unreasonable command and the unbearable heat being generated by the furnace, they were incinerated. Even so, the three men tumbled in, bound with ropes, to their doom.

We know, because we've read the story, that they walked out unscathed. We know how Nebuchadnezzar, after sitting back to watch them burn, "jumped up in alarm" and blurted out to those around him, "Didn't we throw three men, bound, into the fire?" (Dan. 3:24).

"Yes, of course, Your Majesty," his advisers answered (3:24).

But Nebuchadnezzar just pointed. "Look! I see four men, not tied, walking around in the fire unharmed; and the fourth looks like a son of the gods" (3:25).

"There is no other god who is able to deliver like this," Nebuchadnezzar exclaimed when Shadrach, Meshach, and Abednego emerged from the furnace (3:29). He was simply overwhelmed by the fact that this God had "sent his angel and rescued his servants who trusted in him" (3:28). And so he issued a decree that no one in the kingdom could bother the three men ever again.

The simplest way to interpret this story, the most obvious rationale for why it ends with Nebuchadnezzar *again* praising "the God of Shadrach, Meshach, and Abednego" (3:28)—is that he'd just seen three men thrown into the furnace and then emerge with not even a hair on their heads singed, with not even the smell of smoke on their unburned clothing. That would get the attention of even the most stubborn, callous observer.

But really, I believe, it was the whole day's events that led to that outcome. It was the daring courage of three men, out of a mass of thousands, who realized they were no longer in control of their day but were still in control of their worship—and they would not relinquish that under any conditions. They didn't try to negotiate a workable compromise. They didn't try to justify the act of physically bowing as polite accommodation to their hosts at the event, even as they

> When we worship and serve God alone; when we refuse to bow to earthly kings, powers, ideologies, and systems; when we refuse to allow interruptions, inconveniences, and unwelcome circumstances to bury us in frustration and self-pity, we open the door for God's power and glory to shine through.

silently worshiped God in their hearts. No, this was a clear-cut matter to them. They bowed their knee to God, only to God. At all times, in all places.

Then it was the way they spoke to the king: *We don't need to caucus about whether your death sentence will cause us to reconsider. God will save us or He will not, but He is God either way. Full stop.* Their tone reminds me of Job responding to the chiding of his counselors after finding himself in such unspeakable depths of suffering, with God seemingly unwilling to come to his rescue: "Even if he kills me, I will hope in him" (Job 13:15). If you believe in a God who rules and who raises the dead, you can afford to talk that way, even if the man or woman who's listening is the most powerful human you know.

And finally, more important, it was the "fourth" Man in the flames. Nebuchadnezzar thought he was seeing an angel or "a son of the gods." But in reality this individual was surely *the* "Son of God"—Jesus Himself who, whatever our predicament, responds to our faith by coming into our furnace, absorbing the judgment made against us, ministering to our hearts, and walking *with us* through the fire. (Most commentators believe the figure in the flames was a Christophany, a preincarnate appearance of Christ on the earth.)

Shadrach, Meshach, and Abednego had no guarantee they would escape the conflagration that the events of the day had created for them. Neither do we. But whatever the end result, Jesus will be there ahead of us, either to rescue us or to take us to glory with Him.

It's a testimony either way.

Sometimes our greatest witness to God's reality and power happens when we suffer affliction and trials, when others see us trusting Him and not being swallowed up by the ordeal. That can be a more powerful witness than never being thrown into the furnace in the first place. Or into the lions' den. Or into whatever modern-day crucible might be seeking to overcome us today.

When we worship and serve God alone; when we refuse to bow to earthly kings, powers, ideologies, and systems; when we refuse to allow interruptions, inconveniences, and unwelcome circumstances to bury us in frustration and self-pity, we set the stage. We open the door for God's power and glory to shine through. We cooperate with Him in lighting a path so that even those who've rejected or marginalized Him may see that He truly is the way, the truth, and the life (John 14:6). And the reason they see Him in us—"your God," "our God," "the God of Shadrach, Meshach, and Abednego"—is because *we* see Him as our Ruler over everything that touches us.

Many are the times in recent years that Robert and I have prayed before entering another medical office or hospital room, "Lord, may we walk and react and live and love in such a way that people see You in us." In every situation, no matter how stressful or difficult, we want people to see, know, and worship "the God of Robert and Nancy."

Only Heaven knows how far-reaching and transformational will be the testimony of those who truly believe that Heaven rules.

CHAPTER FIVE

Humbled

How monotonously alike
all the great tyrants and conquerors have been;
how gloriously different are the saints.

—C.S. Lewis

KING NEBUCHADNEZZAR was dead after a forty-year reign, and Babylon reeled. In Nebuchadnezzar's massive wake, a succession of kings ruled, each for a short period of time. Then came Belshazzar, who equaled Nebuchadnezzar both in the number of z's in his name and in his overall disposition.

The two were much alike. Both Nebuchadnezzar and Belshazzar were idolaters, both extravagant and ostentatious, obsessed with their own wealth and privilege. Both ruled by force and fear, eliminating anyone who got in their way while rewarding anyone who bolstered their ego or supported their regime. Most notably, however, both men held a high—supremely high—view of themselves.

They are portraits of pride.

And pride, in whatever form it takes, is an enemy of Heaven's rule because it keeps us from acknowledging or even seeing the truth about ourselves and God.

Think of how the two monarchs' pride blinded them to some of the bedrock principles we've already observed:

- Pride kept them from seeing that everything they possessed had been given to them by God.
- Pride kept them from seeing that He was the sovereign, supreme power of the world and that they were dependent on Him for their very breath and existence.
- Pride kept them from seeing that the One who'd raised them up could just as easily bring them down, that He controlled not only the reach but also the length of their individual reigns.

Pride can also blind you and me to these important truths—and, more important, keep us from living in them. This invites disaster in more ways than one. Not only does it deprive us of the comfort and courage we are meant to receive from living under Heaven's rule. It also inevitably sets us up for a fall, because Heaven rules whether we acknowledge it or not.

God doesn't rule because we've granted Him permission to do so. He rules simply because of who He is. Certain details might be up for discussion, but His sovereignty is not up for a vote. It's a given, like gravity. The only thing to be determined is not how we'll be affected by it but how we adjust our lives to it:

whether with blinding pride or with eye-opening humility.

And as anyone who seeks to defy gravity will tell you (or wishes they were still around to tell you), the difference can be a matter of life and death.

We've already seen the pride of Nebuchadnezzar. For another living lesson in pride, let's take a look at Daniel 5, which focuses on an incident in the reign of King Belshazzar. In fact, before reading on, why not take a few minutes and read through that chapter yourself. As you do, take note of any expressions and consequences you see of pride—and of humility.

A STUDY IN PRIDE

As Daniel 5 opens, we become uninvited guests at a lavish feast held in Belshazzar's royal honor. It's the only glimpse we're given in Scripture of Babylon under his kingly rule. The wine flows freely, its abundance likely indicative of free-flowing extravagance and moral looseness as well. Most shocking of all, to us, is the king's drunken order to "bring in the gold and silver vessels that his predecessor Nebuchadnezzar had taken from the temple in Jerusalem, so that the king and his nobles, wives, and concubines could drink from them" (Dan. 5:2).

For us as lovers of God's Word, that's hard to read. Even harder to imagine.

The confiscation of these items from the house of Jewish worship had spoken volumes to the Babylonians, both when it took place a generation earlier and continuing through the years. Symbolically it confirmed the triumph of their gods over the Hebrews' God. Because if the God of Israel ruled, as Daniel and others claimed He did, why had so many of His sacred things been walked out of His temple by enemy hands? Why wasn't He able to protect them? Why were they now in storage in the Babylonian palace, where they could be carted out like this for toasts to Babylon's king and also to Babylon's god, Bel, who (the Babylonians believed) gave the king his mighty power and had even given the king his name? (Belshazzar means "Bel save the king.")

Yet remember this moment. Remember pride's moment—*all* the moments we've seen so far in Daniel:

- Nebuchadnezzar's dream about a "colossal statue" made of gold and other metals (Dan. 2)
- the golden statue Nebuchadnezzar built to honor himself, rising ninety feet high and covered with gold (Dan. 3)
- the tree standing tall in Nebuchadnezzar's nighttime vision (Dan. 4)

Then remember that first statue toppling; remember the second statue being trivialized by God's miraculous deliverance from the furnace; remember the tree being cut down, and Nebuchadnezzar, in the aftermath of his great fall, finally coming to his senses, lifting his eyes up to heaven, and saying: "Now I, Nebuchadnezzar, praise, exalt, and glorify the King of the heavens" (4:37).

And now picture this scene on what turned out to be the last night of the reign of Nebuchadnezzar's successor: The gleam of gold when Belshazzar's servants open the closets where the vessels from Jerusalem's temple were kept. The slosh of wine in goblets that had once held pure water in service of the living God and in fulfillment of His ordinances. The clink of sacred vessels being clashed together in debauched disregard for their original intention, carried high upon the revelry of licentious laughter and the hoarse singing of old men.

Envision this moment, when human pride seemed to have triumphed and when God and all that is holy and good seemed to have been trounced. Because these moments are still happening today.

A staff researcher in our ministry sends me a weekly round-up of links to articles on various current events and cultural issues and trends in our world. Each edition highlights scores of such moments. Court rulings, school board decisions, and new legislation that fly in the face of truth and justice. Elected officials, celebrities, and, all-too-often, pastors and Christian leaders who make the headlines by flaunting evil and flouting God's law. Repressive regimes that clamp down on followers of Christ and seek to eliminate gospel witness in the public square.

Pride walks. Everywhere.

But "Heaven rules." Over everything.

God is not losing at anything. The pride that seems to be winning is only awaiting its date with destruction.

And in Daniel 5, God captured this truth in His own handwriting.

As the party atmosphere swelled to its highest crest, suddenly—
"at that moment"—the wild shouts of gluttonous celebration
turned into shrieks of holy terror. Every head turned as "the fin-
gers of a man's hand appeared and began writing on the plaster
of the king's palace wall" (5:5).

Even proud Belshazzar went to pieces. "His face turned pale,
and his thoughts so terrified him that," according to one translation of the Bible, "he soiled himself and his knees knocked
together" (5:6). This man who considered his power absolute
and himself invincible from attack now found himself trembling
before a Power so superior it could demolish all human pride,
even that of earth's most pompous potentates.

Yet human pride isn't easily vanquished. And Belshazzar didn't
tremble for long. Soon this proud king was barking out orders,
calling for his diviners and counselors. Accustomed to buying
his subjects' loyalties, he proudly began offering prizes to anyone
who could decipher what was happening in the room and what
the strange words on the wall could possibly mean (5:7).

Belshazzar refused to relinquish his pride even in the presence
of God's powerful hand. But pride would be the death of him.
And pride, left untreated, will be the death of us as well. It is
always a losing proposition. Pride cannot help but lead to the loss
of those things we somehow think we're controlling by clinging
to them so tightly. Power. Security. Persuasion. Manipulation.

So why do we hold on to our pride? Because pride, despite
its costs, is a resolute, irresistible suitor. Both alluring and decep-
tive, it keeps us convinced that we can't live without it. Maybe

if the only side it showed us was as unbecoming as Belshazzar's blatant conceit, we wouldn't be as susceptible to it. But pride can masquerade in ways that are less offensive and more subtle—yet no less an attempt to stiff-arm Heaven's rule.

Think of it. Being super organized, excelling in school or sports, working longer hours than the rest of our colleagues, keeping a spotless house, having an empty inbox, never running late for an appointment—any of these qualities could be born out of genuine love for God and others . . . or they might reveal an underlying drive to control or to be admired by others. So might coveting and currying recognition as a church leader or a top producer, insisting our position on a

> ∧
>
> Pride cannot help but lead to the loss of those things we somehow think we're controlling.
>
> ∨

controversial matter is "right" and dismissing those who don't see eye to eye, and being overly competitive in sports or business.

Or think about what we call low self-esteem, something that on the face of it could seem to be just the opposite of pride. But might this low sense of self-worth at times be a form of simmering displeasure at how our Creator designed us and intends to display His glory through us? Rather than listen to what He says about us, we listen to the voices that fuel our feelings, the debilitating lies that discount our worth and suffocate our joy. We validate those feelings because of the pain and rejection that may have fed them. We hope to insulate our wounded hearts so as to avoid further hurt. But do we not see the tinge of pride that colors our low view of ourselves, as if we know ourselves better than our loving Creator does? Could this despising of ourselves be at heart a disappointed, disillusioned disbelief of Heaven's rule?

And what about anxiety? Don't we sometimes seek the sense of control it gives us over our circumstances? Over our fears? Over our concern for the well-being of our loved ones? Yet when we're twisted up in our worries, we'll often take them over anything. Even over Heaven's rule.

Robert and I were reminded of the tenacity of this temptation when we received a text from a dear friend in her nineties. She lost her husband to COVID about a year ago, has battled residual effects of COVID herself, and more recently has been diagnosed with breast cancer. Her note detailed some of the challenges she'd been facing, troubles piling up one on top of another with no end in sight. The battle had been wearing on her, she said, especially while trying to get through the holiday season and missing her husband of seventy years, and had left her struggling with fatigue and discouragement.

But "I am finally feeling better," she wrote. "I think anxiety was sapping my strength. It's one thing to *say* things are in God's hands and another thing to think you have to help Him carry them."

Oh, this pull we feel toward thinking we can manage our own lives and shoulder our own burdens. How deceptively cruel is this tactic of our enemy—so enticingly played and yet so dangerous. No matter our stage of life, pride can pilfer our peace and sabotage our trust in heaven's Ruler, hiding behind natural concern for our own well-being and the protective instincts we feel toward our family and friends.

We may not be proud along the order of Belshazzar, but pride can lure us away from the truth by other means as well, by other bandits. May the writing on *our* wall be inscribed in the indelible ink of "Heaven rules," with none of our own ruling demands scribbled over it.

A STUDY IN HUMILITY

We first saw Daniel as a teenage exile, bravely holding to his convictions in the king's court. In Daniel 2 we saw him calmly responding to Nebuchadnezzar's threats after no one could interpret the king's perplexing dreams. In Daniel 4 we saw him again risking the king's displeasure by interpreting a disturbing dream. But though Daniel proved himself capable and faithful in every position he occupied in Babylon, skillful in imparting God's wisdom and truth to those who needed it, it appears he spent a number of years on the sidelines—his words unwanted, his counsel unsought. By the time we come to Daniel 5, he was now likely in his late seventies, serving in yet another godless administration, under yet another proud king, and relegated to irrelevance.

Yet when the hastily assembled "wise men" (Dan. 5:7) in Belshazzar's court failed to come up with a single clue for decoding the words written by the mysterious hand on Belshazzar's wall, someone remembered hearing stories from the past about a guy named Daniel.

"There is a man in your kingdom who has a spirit of the holy gods in him. In the days of your predecessor he was found to have insight, intelligence, and wisdom like the wisdom of the gods . . . an extraordinary spirit, knowledge . . . and the ability to interpret dreams, explain riddles, and solve problems. Therefore, summon Daniel, and he will give the interpretation." (5:11–12)

Mark it: "Heaven rules." By now, time and influence had seemingly passed Daniel by. The people who had once known him and valued his gifts and insight were now long dead or no longer in leadership. He was a relic from a former age, a dim memory from the distant past. And yet there was no hint of bitterness, competitiveness, or hypersensitivity in Daniel. And he was still ready to be of service to the king because he'd stayed in humble service to his real King.

Now if pride was how Daniel operated, certain choices were available to him when the messengers came bearing Belshazzar's emergency call.

He could refuse, offended at how his past contributions had been forgotten. *That's pride.*

He could go with them as ordered but seek to leverage the situation to his own benefit. *That's pride too.* After all, he had them over a barrel. If they wanted his advice badly enough, and if no one else could provide the answers they sought, they could expect to compensate him at whatever price he demanded.

Or he could just be Daniel and come when he was summoned,

trusting that God was at work in the situation. And that, of course, was Daniel's choice.

Oh, the simplicity of humility! When we accept that Heaven rules, we just follow where God leads. Not grudgingly. Not opportunistically. Not irritably or fearfully. Just freely.

Humbly.

It's a beautiful thing to watch.

"Daniel was brought before the king," Scripture tells us. And Belshazzar, having composed himself somewhat and looking more like his usual self, said to him, "Are you Daniel, one of the Judean exiles that my predecessor the king brought from Judah?" (5:13).

"Judean exiles." Hear within this racial reference a note of snobbery, a sneer of derision. And this, too, provided an opening for pride to snap itself onto Daniel's viewfinder—the blinding pride of stirred emotions, of settling scores and registering disgust.

Instead, Daniel kept his head clear, his spirit watchful, as Belshazzar launched into a monologue filled with equal parts flattery and bribery—his royal mode of operation, the way he typically got things done in his kingdom. "If you can read this inscription and give me its interpretation," he said, "you will be clothed in purple, have a gold chain around your neck, and have the third highest position in the kingdom" (5:16).

The pressure was on. Or was it?

Not when humility was at work. Because Daniel's humility—his clear understanding of who he was and what his God could do—enabled his quiet confidence.

You see, humility is how we appropriate the full blessings and real-time benefits of Heaven's rule. It's the doorway God uses to overwhelm us, far beyond our own understanding, with the gifts of His comfort and His courage.

I think that's part of what Jesus was talking about when He gave the heads-up to His first-century followers about events that would one day become commonplace in their experience.

"You will be brought before kings and governors because of my name," he told them (Luke 21:12). They would find themselves in places where a person who craves control will feel undone, places where those whose pride feeds on approval will want to say whatever makes them look good. But "make up your minds not to prepare your defense ahead of time," Jesus instructed them—and us—"for I will give you such words and a wisdom that none of your adversaries will be able to resist or contradict" (vv. 14–15).

> /\
> Humility is how we appropriate the full blessings and real-time benefits of Heaven's rule. It's the doorway God uses to overwhelm us, far beyond our own understanding, with the gifts of His comfort and His courage.
> \/

What Jesus was describing is a "Heaven rules" moment as well as a humility moment—not thinking too much of ourselves, not thinking too little of ourselves, but simply not thinking of ourselves, thinking only of how God is ruling over us and over every situation we encounter. How liberating and energizing is this perpetual HR walk of faith.

This is what we see in Daniel—and what we can expect to see in ourselves as we put to death the pride that seeks to keep us on the throne and tether our hearts and minds to the reality of Heaven's rule.

Hear it in his response to King Belshazzar: "You may keep your gifts and give your rewards to someone else." *I'm not here for the money or to make a name for myself.* "However, I will read the inscription for the king and make the interpretation known to him" (5:17).

Daniel could serve his earthly king without prideful motives because he served his heavenly King from a humble heart. What could Belshazzar give him that he needed or didn't already possess? You can't have any better position than being a servant of the Most High God. So what did Daniel stand to lose by being fearlessly loyal to heaven's Ruler in this challenging moment? He was free to speak truth to power without angling for personal advantage or fearing public recrimination.

Completely humble, because Heaven rules.

But what about the proud king of Babylon? Read the writing on the wall (or Daniel's interpretation of it):

- "God has numbered the days of your kingdom and brought it to an end" (5:26).
- "You have been weighed on the balance and found deficient" (5:27).
- "Your kingdom has been divided and given to the Medes and Persians" (5:28).

Why was all this happening? Because *"you . . . Belshazzar,* have not humbled your heart,"* but instead "have exalted yourself against the Lord of the heavens."

> "The vessels from [God's] house were brought to you,
> and as you and your nobles, wives, and concubines drank
> wine from them, you praised the gods made of silver and
> gold, bronze, iron, wood, and stone, which do not see or
> hear or understand. But you have not glorified the God
> who holds your life-breath in his hand and who controls
> the whole course of your life [*Heaven rules!*]. Therefore,
> he sent the hand, and this writing was inscribed."
> (5:22–24)

Humility and pride. They are light and darkness, life and death. That's why we must choose to be ruled not by ourselves— *never* by ourselves—but by the One who has our "life-breath in his hand," the One apart from whom we could not survive the next five seconds.

This is a pride-killing truth to those who truly want to live.

A humility-inducing truth to those who truly want to learn.

And a life-giving truth to those who truly want to be free.

But what if we choose wrongly? We've already seen that pride can blind us to the truth. So what happens when we finally open our eyes and realize we've allowed our pride to hold us captive and lead us toward destruction?

Because of God's mercy, repentance is still a choice we can make.

A STUDY IN MERCY

"This is so that the living will know
that the Most High is ruler
over human kingdoms." (Dan. 4:17)

This is what the angel said to proud King Nebuchadnezzar in his second dream, the one Daniel interpreted as predicting the king's humbling downfall. As we've seen, the dream came true, and the king was indeed brought low. But as a result he finally acknowledged Heaven's rule.

If Nebuchadnezzar was sincere, he ended up exactly where God wants all of us to be. Aligned with the truth of His rule. Trusting His ways and His wisdom. Walking boldly and confidently wherever He sends us. Comforted and encouraged as we are held by His guiding hand.

Here is our safety. Here is our usefulness. Here is our opportunity to follow His will, to find contentment, and to be free from feeling we have to bear the weight of the world, trusting our good and generous Father to be responsible for all those things we have mistakenly thought *we* were responsible for.

This is living. This is blessing. This is grace.

So will you go there with Him? Will you step out on this journey with Him? Better yet, if pride has been clouding your trust and willingness to believe in the goodness of God and in where He wants you to go with Him—will you open your eyes and see?

There's mercy for that. The mercy of God. The power of repentance. The promise of change.

It's humbling, yes—in a good way, in a decluttering way, in a twenty-pounds-lighter way. And yet humility is also a difficult choice for us humans, and God knows this. He made us, and He understands us. He knows how tightly we grip those things we look to for security. He knows our reluctance to let go. He knows how hard it is for us to trust Him to run this world. And He knows the reason we build such fortresses of pride around ourselves anyway is usually to mask our hidden fears and insecurities.

So He is patient. He's willing to make this a process. If the place we're going is humility, He will take the time to walk it out with us. He'll even put us in the right conditions to steer us there, toward being right-minded. Toward having a right-sized view of ourselves. In agreement with reality. At peace.

God was even merciful with Belshazzar. I know his demise may seem sudden and abrupt, and in a sense it was. But if we listen closely to the message God gave him through Daniel, we see divine mercy. We see patience. We see it that Belshazzar was given multiple opportunities to learn humility. He just chose to ignore them.

Amazingly, those opportunities came through the unlikely example of Belshazzar's predecessor, King Nebuchadnezzar.

Remember what Nebuchadnezzar was like? Remember him ordering the execution of all his counselors? Remember him later ordering the execution of Shadrach, Meshach, and Abednego? Remember him ordering the furnace kindled to seven times its usual heat, making it impossible for anyone to survive such a fiery command from such an empowered ruler?

Belshazzar no doubt remembered or had heard the stories of Nebuchadnezzar's notorious pride. In case he'd forgotten, Daniel refreshed his memory:

> "Because of the greatness [God] gave [Nebuchadnezzar], all peoples, nations, and languages were terrified and fearful of him. He killed anyone he wanted and kept alive anyone he wanted; he exalted anyone he wanted and humbled anyone he wanted." (Dan. 5:19)

Isn't that right, Belshazzar? Remember? Isn't that how you remember him?

Surely the king remembered hearing the story of Nebuchadnezzar's dream—the great tree cut down, leaving only a stump. *Isn't that what happened, Belshazzar? Remember?*

The Lord (again in mercy, again in patience) had given Nebuchadnezzar time to change, to reorient his heart and life around heaven's rule. In fact, God had waited a full year after delivering the interpretation of that dream before carrying out His discipline against the proud king. Not until twelve months later, while Nebuchadnezzar was out enjoying the view of his city from the roof of his palatial home, lost in grandiose thoughts about himself and his successes, had God moved to humble him.

Remember what Nebuchadnezzar said? Do you hear the prideful "me" message in his words?

> "Is this not Babylon the Great that *I have built* to be a royal residence by *my vast power* and for *my majestic glory*?" (4:30)

Remember, Belshazzar?

> "When [Nebuchadnezzar's] heart was exalted and his spirit became arrogant, he was deposed from his royal throne and his glory was taken from him. He was driven away from people, his mind was like an animal's, he lived with the wild donkeys, he was fed grass like cattle, and his body was drenched with dew from the sky until . . ." (5:20–21)

Until what, Belshazzar?

> ". . . until he acknowledged that the Most High God is ruler over human kingdoms and sets anyone he wants over them." (5:21)

Isn't that right, Belshazzar? Do you remember? "You knew all this" (5:22). Yet you didn't humble yourself.

Nebuchadnezzar's story was meant as a mercy—a cautionary tale to warn those who would occupy the throne in years to come. That's why Belshazzar's fall, which was complete before the day was over—"That very night [he] was killed" (5:30)—was not heartless judgment but the result of mercy refused.

And so here we sit today, either somewhere in the process of humbling ourselves before the rule and Ruler of heaven or else resisting Him, retreating from Him, afraid to let go of our darling pride.

We've been shown the way. We've been given the promises. We've been exposed to a myriad of examples of people taken down by their pride. As Psalm 91:7 says, we've seen "a thousand fall at [our] side," maybe as many as "ten thousand at [our] right hand," each one deceived by the same sinful pattern of worshiping themselves, exalting their own desires, pridefully refusing to live under anyone else's rule.

But

> the one who lives under the protection of the Most High
> dwells in the shadow of the Almighty. (Ps. 91:1)

And He, the Most High God, is calling us by His mercy to come live there, humbled beneath His glory yet exalted by our union with Him into true greatness.

Did Nebuchadnezzar really get to a place of genuine change and repentance? We don't know for sure. The last we heard from him, he was at least saying the right things, honoring the Most High and seeing himself in a truer light:

> All the inhabitants of the earth are counted as nothing,
> and he does what he wants with the army of heaven
> and the inhabitants of the earth.

There is no one who can block his hand
or say to him, "What have you done?". . . (Dan. 4:35)

Now I, Nebuchadnezzar, praise, exalt, and glorify the
King of the heavens, because all his works are true and
his ways are just. He is able to humble those who walk in
pride. (4:37)

Yes, believe it or not, that's King Nebuchadnezzar talking.
And maybe it's how Nebuchadnezzar actually lived out the
remaining years of his life. I hope so. We know that the Lord
restored his kingdom to him, giving him "even more greatness"
than he'd previously had (4:36). And we know God that gave
him time and mercy to repent, just as He patiently gives time
and mercy to us—not to take us down but to take us up.

"Whoever exalts himself will be humbled, and whoever
humbles himself will be exalted." (Matt. 23:12)

Humble yourselves, therefore, under the mighty hand of
God, so that he may exalt you at the proper time.
(1 Peter 5:6)

And what if we don't? What if we don't humble ourselves
under God's hand? What if we cling to our proud thoughts and
ways? That last sentence of Nebuchadnezzar's address after he
turned from his pride and was restored from his years of insanity
never fails to speak to my heart:

He is able to humble those who walk in pride.
(Dan. 4:37)

It's a frightful thing to resist Heaven's rule. Those who do may seem to prevail—for a time. But in the end, well, Heaven still rules.

You and I need this reminder. We need it for ourselves when we are walking in unrepentant, self-deluded pride. God is able to humble us. And He will, if we refuse to humble ourselves.

We also need this reminder when we see others walking in unrepentant pride—whether they are the leaders, influencers, and celebrities we watch on the news or the people we live and work with each day. God is able to humble them, too—and He will, if they refuse to humble themselves.

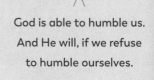

God is able to humble us. And He will, if we refuse to humble ourselves.

But we must keep in mind that humbling others is His job, not ours. Because our own pride can cause us to accentuate the evil in others while being blind to the evil in our own hearts.

I'll be honest: There's a Nebuchadnezzar in my heart. There's probably a Nebuchadnezzar in yours too. The *proud* Nebuchadnezzar.

"My power."

"My glory."

"My way."

"My decisions."

"My ideas."

"My control."

"My hard work."

"My opinions."

How thankful I am that there's mercy to help us lay these things down, to lift our eyes up, and to see the kind of life that could be ours by choosing the health of humility over the sickness of pride. To help us surrender our drive to rule our own lives (and others' lives) and to humbly embrace Heaven's rule.

CHAPTER SIX

Look Up!

God knows His plan,
and even when He reveals His plan to us,
He expects us to pray over that plan.

—*Dr. David Jeremiah*

AS A RETIRED MARINE CORPS sergeant who had served in combat during Operation Desert Storm, Joe Kennedy had a lot to offer the high school football team he was hired to coach in 2008: discipline, toughness, devotion to duty, a no-quit attitude. He's still teaching those things today.

Only not as a football coach.

That's because before he ever put a whistle around his neck, Joe made a commitment. Inspired by a faith-based movie he'd seen before his first season on the sideline (*Facing the Giants,* by Christian filmmakers Alex and Stephen Kendrick), he promised God that after every game, no matter the outcome, he would express thanks to Him by offering a prayer before he left the field. It would be his simple testimony to what mattered most to him—to what matters most in life. A simple acknowledgment that the opportunity to coach young men was a blessing given to him from the God of heaven, from whom all blessings flow.

Throughout seven seasons, at the conclusion of every contest, Coach Kennedy would walk by himself to the fifty-yard line, take a knee, and for no more than fifteen seconds, bow his head in a simple prayer.

Over the years a small handful of his players—often a number of the opposing team's players as well—would voluntarily join Joe in that brief moment. In fact, a compliment paid to him by an administrator from another school is what first brought Coach Kennedy's low-key postgame prayer ritual to the attention of his own school administration. They warned him to stop or alter this practice, saying it violated church-and-state regulations. Unwilling to comply, he was eventually given an ultimatum. He would either do his praying where nobody could see him, or else he would find himself looking for another job.

The next Friday night, after the completion of their game, Coach Kennedy took his usual walk to the center of the playing field and offered his usual prayer. By the following Friday night, he'd been relieved of his coaching duties.

So Daniel lives. It can still happen. The verdict can come down, and the lions may await. But no matter how many school boards and judges and appeals courts continue making their infamous rulings, there is one Ruler in heaven who outranks them. One who outranks all of us.

Daniel's God still presides.

And God's people still pray.

UNSTOPPABLE PRAYER

If prayer is a struggle for you, as it is for me, you've probably asked yourself: Why is consistent prayer such an effort? Why are my prayers so tepid and forced? Why do they seldom feel effective? Why is there so little passion and power behind them, unlike the way other people's praying often sounds?

There's no single key that turns us from spotty prayers to unstoppable prayers. But here's what I've found, and am finding, as I strive to keep my focus on Heaven's rule as it intersects with my day. If deep down I believe that earthly people and earthly forces rule—governments, critics, decision makers, societal trends—if I think they're the ones who carry the most weight and influence over my life and my world, I'll spend most of my thinking and energy on them: how to change minds, how to fight back, how to defend my actions, how to get people to like me. I'll want to impress those who can do something for me. I'll tend to fret over the ones who are upset with me. I'll want to run from situations that are knotty, messy, and complicated. I'll want to just go work a crossword puzzle or watch Netflix or something, anything, to dull the angst in my soul.

But if I really believe that Heaven rules . . .

Help me finish that sentence. Write this paragraph with me. Tailor it to the specifics of your own life and your own sense of being bombarded by people who, perhaps right now, are making demands on you (whether fair or unfair), or taking advantage of your kindness and generosity, or insisting you agree with their version of reality, or deciding whether to award you a scholarship or accept your offer on their house. If those people rule, you'd better be investing every ounce of yourself into getting them into your corner or off your back, whichever outcome applies to whichever person.

But because Heaven rules, the always-appropriate response is to pray. To talk with the One who does rule. To ask of Him what you believe is right and receive from Him what He knows is best. To place your life in His hands and trust that you can be in no safer place and find no more reliable provision. In prayer we can know we've been heard, and we can experience the calm and courage that carry and steady us when every other remedy has done nothing but deplete us.

Yes, when we understand that Heaven rules, even our prayer life changes.

Or, as in Daniel's case, refuses to change.

Got your Bible open? In this chapter we're going to look at three scenes from Daniel's prayer life. To lay the groundwork, read Daniel 2:17–19, 6:1–10, and 9:1–23. How would you describe Daniel's prayers? What connection do you see in these passages between the conviction that Heaven rules and the prayers of God's people?

A HABIT OF PRAYER

The overnight demise of Belshazzar not only meant a new king on the throne but a whole new power structure in place. It wasn't just Belshazzar that fell; Babylon fell. Nebuchadnezzar's dream about the multitiered statue, with himself and his empire as the "head of gold" to be overtaken by the "silver," by the rise of another geopolitical body, was playing out in real time on the world stage. The "very night Belshazzar the king of the Chaldeans was killed," the Bible says, "Darius the Mede received the kingdom at the age of sixty-two" (Dan. 5:30–31).

New sheriff in town. A new superpower on top.

So you can imagine what people were talking about on the street, what was on most people's minds and took front and center place in most of their conversations. It's not unlike what happens when a new administration takes over in Washington or when the company you work for is bought out and a new team of managers are brought in. Everybody wonders what this new day will be like, how the new regime will change things, and how the change will affect them personally.

This doesn't, however, seem to be where Daniel's train of thought was going. While everyone else's attention was turned toward the new king, Darius, Daniel's eyes were fixed on the King who ruled from heaven. That's what mattered most to him.

I'm not saying he wasn't interested in the news or in keeping up with which way the imperial winds were blowing. He certainly was aware that Darius the Mede, like the kings of Babylon before him, struck an intimidating pose—definitely "large and in charge." According to Medo-Persian custom, the king was infallible. His royal decrees could not be repealed by any act or movement of the people, not even by the king himself. It therefore behooved everyone to stay heads-up on his statements and actions, to follow closely each day's version of the Persian press.

But Daniel's primary method for keeping up with what truly made a difference in the world was a practice the world knows little about and understands even less. Three times a day, we're told, regular as clockwork, he would go to his house (if he wasn't there already), ascend to an upstairs room where the open windows faced southward toward Jerusalem, get down on his knees, and pray.

/\

Your prayer life will reveal what you really believe.

\/

Now, you can't keep that up for a lifetime, as Daniel did, much less for a week, a month, or a year, unless you're convinced that Heaven rules. And you can't pray like that if you don't believe the rule of Heaven is the real determinant of what happens to you and how it affects your life here on earth and, more important, for eternity. You can testify all you want, but your prayer life will reveal what you really believe.

And Daniel's prayer life did just that. We've seen it all along. Think back to those tense hours in Daniel 2, after the summons had been sent out ordering the mass execution of all the men responsible for giving Nebuchadnezzar counsel. The king had experienced a distressing dream; he couldn't remember it; he demanded that his team of toadies remember it for him. And when they couldn't—because who could?—Daniel found himself in hot water through no fault of his own.

Clearly this was a time to act. For most people that would have meant a time to scramble—whether to attempt armed resistance or just flee for the hills. Instead, Daniel ran to those three close friends of his—Hananiah, Mishael, and Azariah, better known to us by their Babylonian names, Shadrach, Meshach, and Abednego—"urging them to ask the God of the heavens for mercy concerning this mystery" of the king's dream so that they "would not be destroyed with the rest of Babylon's wise men" (Dan. 2:18).

They prayed. They asked. And when God answered, when He made the "mystery" known to Daniel, what did Daniel do? What would you and I have done? I imagine, knowing time was of the essence, knowing our necks were on the line, we'd likely have dashed immediately to the king and spilled to him everything the Lord had just told us. But Daniel, instead, stopped to praise "the God of the heavens" (2:19). Not just with a quick thanks. Not with a wink and a nod on his way out the door. He stayed there in extended praise—four rich verses in our Bibles. And only after praying and praising did he seek out the man who held the ax in his hand and request an appointment with the king.

That's the snapshot we're given in Scripture of Daniel's prayer habits as a younger man. It explains a lot about how he developed his spirit of wisdom, the insight he possessed about matters that confounded almost everyone else. It also explains a lot about how he could keep from panicking under pressure and about how he remained gracious and humble in his reactions and demeanor even up into his seventies and eighties.

IN THE SCHOOL OF PRAYER

We know that God moves in response to the prayers, humility, and repentance of His people to accomplish His purposes in our world. We believe that our prayers matter. But how can we learn to pray more effectively?

One way is by hearing other people pray—people who don't pray just casual or hurried prayers, but people like Daniel who pour out their hearts to the God of heaven because they know Him, love Him, and believe He rules.

Daniel, in fact, has a lot to teach us about prayer. Daniel 9 records one of the longest, most earnest prayers in Scripture, offered up by Daniel at the outset of the Medo-Persian takeover. (For the fullest impact, follow along in your Bible as we overview this moving example of intercessory prayer.)

By the time Darius came to power, Daniel had lived his whole long life in a place he would not have chosen if it had been up to him, dealing with horrific problems, answering to horrific rulers, maneuvering around horrific public policies, and witnessing horrific persecution against his friends and his people. But "in the first year of Darius" (Dan. 9:1), instead of checking out, instead of retiring, instead of being too cynical and weary to try adjusting to another change, Daniel remained focused on those things that never change.

And how did he keep himself focused? For starters, *he went to the Scriptures.* I love this.

> In the first year of [Darius'] reign, I, Daniel, understood
> from the books according to the word of the LORD to
> the prophet Jeremiah that the number of years for the
> desolation of Jerusalem would be seventy. (9:2)

Think about that.

While everyone else's attention was turned toward the new administration, Daniel's eyes were fixed on the Most High God and His kingdom. He was eager to know what God had to say about the days in which he was living.

But how could he know that? The same way we can know. Many of us get our knowledge of what's going on in the world by listening to friends or watching cable news or reading social media posts. But Daniel got his briefings and perspective by looking up—by reading the Word of God.

Think about the fact that Daniel, our Daniel, was able to lay eyes on the same writings of Jeremiah that are right there in your Bible today, where your own eyes and fingertips and highlighter pens have been. Feel the connection of God's people across millennia. Begin to sense, even in this relatively small way, the eternity our God exists in, which He's created us to experience with Him. Sit down with Daniel in the same room for a moment as he reads from passages we know today by their chapter numbers, places like Jeremiah 25 and 29, as the truth begins to dawn on him that God's chosen people have not been forgotten but are living inside the fulfillment of these prophecies.

The passage Daniel read in Jeremiah spoke of how the captivity of the Jews—their removal from Jerusalem—would last for seventy years. By Daniel's reckoning, this seventy-year period was nearing its end. The God who had orchestrated their exile according to His Word, was soon to orchestrate their return—again, according to His Word.

Daniel's response? *He prayed.* His first reaction to God's revealing this truth to him, to having his eyes opened to see heaven's perspective on these current events, was to go to prayer.

> I turned my attention to the Lord God to seek him by prayer and petitions, with fasting, sackcloth, and ashes. (Dan. 9:3)

Prayer requires being willing to turn our attention away from whatever concerns may be pressing in on us, setting aside unnecessary distractions, turning our focus to the Lord.

Notice, too, that Daniel didn't passively sit back and wait for God to fulfill His Word. (The Jewish exiles would in fact return to their homeland just a few years later.) Inspired by the promises of God, Daniel actively humbled himself and prayed.

He began with *praise.* "Ah, Lord—the great and awe-inspiring

> Prayer requires being willing to turn our attention away from whatever concerns may be pressing in on us, turning our focus to the Lord.

God who keeps his gracious covenant with those who love him and keep his commands . . ." (9:4). His focus was Godward. He exalted the covenant-keeping character of God. The person who praises first, before anything else, right-sizes their perspectives by getting themselves right-sized about the nature and character, the majesty and faithfulness, of God.

Daniel's praise led to *confession.* When we see God's greatness and grace, we see ourselves more clearly. Daniel's worship led him to pray, "We have sinned" (9:5). There's the heart of Daniel. Notice that he made no mention of the sins of the Babylonians, the sins of the Medes, the sins of the Persians. And believe me, those people had plenty of sins he could have talked about. But that's not what's important when you have a humble heart and are praying for heaven's perspective.

So Daniel confessed on behalf of his people, God's people: "We have not sought the favor of the LORD our God by turning from our iniquities and paying attention to your truth" (9:13). Sin is how they'd gotten into this mess to begin with. Only by admitting it, learning from it, and repenting of it would they align themselves with the God who'd promised their deliverance.

After confessing, Daniel *pleaded with God to show mercy.* God. had done it before, delivering His people from Egypt, bringing them out "with a strong hand," making His name "renowned as it is this day" (9:15). Would He do it again? It was worth praying for. (After all, there was that promise he'd read in the book of Jeremiah.)

> Lord, in keeping with all your righteous acts, may your
> anger and wrath turn away from your city Jerusalem,
> your holy mountain. . . . Make your face shine on your
> desolate sanctuary. . . . Open your eyes and see our
> desolations and the city that bears your name. . . . Lord,
> hear! Lord, forgive! Lord, listen and act! My God, for
> your own sake, do not delay, because your city and your
> people bear your name. (9:16–19)

Daniel knew his people didn't deserve God's mercy. Far from it. So he appealed to God to show mercy "for your own sake," acknowledging, in effect, "This isn't about us, it's about You!"

Where are the men and women today who know how to pray this way? Why don't *I* pray this way, knowing the desperate condition of God's people and knowing the gracious promises of God?

The rest of Daniel 9 (vv. 20–27) reveals heaven's answer to Daniel's prayer. "While I was praying, Gabriel . . . gave me this explanation" (9:21–22).

"While I was praying." What if Daniel hadn't prayed? What if he had just read Jeremiah's prophecy and moved on to the next thing? You see, prayer was the next thing for Daniel. And it was while he was praying that the answer came from God.

The answer, brought by the angel Gabriel, was that God had heard Daniel's prayer. He would do as Daniel had asked—on His own timetable. In the meantime, the angel said, God's people should not grow discouraged; they should persevere and place their hope in the promises of God. And the same applies to you and me. We, too, must endure through the difficulties, clinging in faith to Him who has promised that one day all wrongs will be righted and all things will be redeemed and made new.

The days in which we live are no less complex than what Daniel faced in his day. Thankfully, we can turn, as he did, to the Word of God, to learn what we need to know, what we should expect, and how we ought to think and live. May our study of Scripture, like Daniel's, move us to prayer—earnest, prevailing prayer. And may our prayers, like Daniel's, be grounded in and fueled by God's Word. This process will anchor our minds and hearts in gospel truth, fill us with hope, and give us His message to share with our generation.

PRAYERS FOR THE LIONS' DEN

Of all the stories in Daniel that have been captured in the watercolors of our childhood memories, the story of "Daniel and the Lions' Den" is almost surely the most beloved, the one we can most easily recall. But that story is not just for the children's Bible storybooks, there to be told and retold at a certain distance, with a certain suspension of reality, having known the ending so well for so many years.

The lions' den is a tale for grownups, too—for us who've been told much in Scripture about the way things will end, how God will ultimately make visible His rule over heaven and earth. But here in the middle of it, in the meantime, in the now-but-not-yet, what are we to do? What will He require us to go through?

We don't always know—except that we're to be faithful, prayerful, and watchful.

This is Daniel's example to us. Head back with me to Daniel 6, where we see that he became the target of a jealous conspiracy by some of his fellow government officials. They carried out their design so craftily that he ended up with no recourse but to let them win—or so it seemed.

His rivals, unable to find any dirt on him, resorted to a strategy that would force him to choose between his loyalty to his God and his loyalty to the king and the empire. They went as a group to King Darius and suggested that he, as a further consolidation of his power, "enforce an edict that, for thirty days, anyone who petitions any god or man except you, the king, will be thrown into the lions' den" (Dan. 6:7).

Naturally the king was amenable to this idea. He gave it his imprimatur, signing it with the same proud flourish that accompanied every "law of the Medes and Persians," meaning it was "irrevocable and [could not] be changed" (6:8).

As often happens, however, with such hasty decisions, his ruling came with an unintended consequence. Despite his penchant for bluster and self-importance, Darius rather liked and leaned on Daniel, the wise and trustworthy Judean. Daniel, by his "extraordinary spirit," had "distinguished himself" from all the others who held positions of leadership in the empire, enough that "the king planned to set him over the whole realm" (6:3) as his right-hand man.

Daniel, therefore, had a lot to lose by not complying with this new ruling, which quite deliberately (by his enemies) yet unintentionally (by the king) made his practice of praying to God a capital offense.

But, as we saw in his encounter with King Belshazzar not too long ago, did Daniel really have anything to lose?

Not if Heaven rules!

This is how we must condition ourselves to think. The truth is

> The truth is stronger than the risk. The Word is louder than the noise. The end is more certain than the present. And God is ruler over all.

stronger than the risk. The Word is louder than the noise. The end is more certain than the present. And God is ruler over all. You and I face many challenges, many distractions, many critical junctures in life where expediency and a drive for self-preservation seem to override what some ancient, Old Testament story would indicate is our best and only choice.

If we want to continue this exhausting dance for people's acceptance and approval, if we believe our hopes are best pinned on the promises other people have made to us and we don't want to do anything to lose them, then let's just keep letting earth rule us.

Let's see how that will turn out. Let's look around when we're sixty or seventy or eighty and discover how little of any real significance we've acquired by thinking our survival depended on appeasing temporary tyrants. Worse, let's reduce the testimony of our lives to how we went along, how we played the game, when God gave us opportunities to shine forth His name by being different from the crowd.

Or let's "dare to be a Daniel," as the children's song goes. Let's turn from listening to what the earth and its screechy voices tell us we're supposed to think and believe—how we're supposed to live and operate if we hope to make it in this world—and let's take Daniel's faithful, determined, unshaken walk home to his upstairs room, to those windows facing open to heaven, to those floorboards where he bowed his knees.

Prayer is where "Heaven rules" lives and breathes. And overcomes.

And let us pray as Daniel did.

Daniel knew his fate was in God's hands, not the king's hands . . . so he prayed.

He knew his God was (and is) more powerful than any earthly power . . . so he prayed.

He knew his God was (and is) the One who hears and answers prayer . . . so he prayed.

He knew the safest place on earth was (is) in God's presence . . . so he prayed.

Prayer is where "Heaven rules" lives and breathes.

And overcomes.

No, it doesn't always look that way. The people who were determined to catch Daniel praying to his God in the privacy of his own home found all the evidence they were looking for. They hurried to report him to King Darius as being in direct violation of the thirty-day order whose ink was still drying in the royal drafting room. And the king, foolishly bound by his own edict, reluctantly raised his hand and gave the command that Daniel be fed to the lions.

So, yes, in the moment, as in most of our moments, there was no visible evidence of "overcoming." To the contrary, things were actually getting worse. There was no way out.

But let's reach back and bring forward some of the HR principles and applications we've been gathering along the way. Let's watch them at work in this unworkable situation and see how they can apply as overcoming strategies in our own lives.

HR STRATEGY #1: **Don't panic—pray!**

King Darius was a ball of nerves the minute he walked away from the lions' den, perhaps scrubbing at the wax left behind on his signet ring from where he'd sealed the order to trap Daniel inside. He couldn't eat, couldn't sleep. Whatever he tried to do, he found no source of relief. He paced, wandered, and fidgeted all night long, checking the window every five minutes to see if dawn was breaking, when he could justify a kingly visit to the execution site and find out what had become of his unlikely Hebrew friend.

Yet tellingly, there's no hint of panic from the man who was actually inside the lions' den, where all the fangs and claws were located. Through it all Daniel remained steady and calm.

Why? The Bible doesn't spell it out, but I imagine Daniel spending the night communing with God in prayer. Perhaps he prayed the words of Psalm 22, which he likely knew well:

> Save me from the lion's mouth. . . . [and]
> I will proclaim your name to my brothers and sisters;
> I will praise you in the assembly.
> You who fear the LORD, praise him! . . .
> For he has not despised or abhorred
> the torment of the oppressed.
> He did not hide his face from him
> but listened when he cried to him for help.
> (vv. 21–24)

HR STRATEGY #2: **Let your prayer be a testimony.**

From the instant Daniel was lowered into the lions' den, he could hear the muffled, echoed words of the king, anxiously begging, "May your God, whom you continually serve, rescue you!" (Dan. 6:16).

Did King Darius really believe this? Did he have even a scrap of faith that Daniel's God could deliver a person enclosed with wild, hungry beasts? Probably not. But he knew what he'd seen in Daniel, who had done nothing but "continually serve" this God. And the king certainly knew what his eyes were telling him about a man so devoted to his God that he would not stop praying, even if it meant the death penalty.

The next morning, when first light had pinked enough of the

sky for Darius to venture out, he raced unroyally to the scene and "cried out in anguish to Daniel. 'Daniel, servant of the living God . . . has your God, whom you continually serve, been able to rescue you from the lions?'" (6:20).

I don't quite know how to adequately describe the incongruity of this picture. Darius couldn't have believed he'd hear a living voice replying to his question. Yet something he'd seen in that "extraordinary spirit" of Daniel sparked enough faith inside this pagan despot—whose own absolute power had not been capable of saving his friend from the lions—to make him believe that Daniel's God might be the One who could pull it off.

That's testimony, my friend. And that's what Daniel's life exuded, so that here in his most critical trial, rather than curse the adversity, he could walk with a confidence in God that messed with even the mixed-up theology of a Medo-Persian monarch.

And so can we. The way you and I walk through such valleys of the shadow of death can result in equal heights of witness today. Believe it!

HR STRATEGY #3: **Keep a "Heaven rules" perspective.**

Prayer helps us see heaven's perspective on earth's events. Through earth's viewfinder, this whole dramatic setup was earmarked for the elimination of Daniel, the promotion of his accusers, and the continuance of cruelty across the empire. But Heaven had other designs.

As we know, not every faithful walk in times of crisis results in the shutting of lions' mouths. For reasons known only to Him, God sometimes allows the lions to prevail. Yet either way, God advances His eternal kingdom through our earthly lives as we put our trust in Him and not in what we can see and hear around us.

In Daniel's case, Heaven's intervention was dramatic and visible to all. Not only did God cause Daniel to make it through the night unharmed; the ones who'd cooked up this conspiracy were thrown into the lions' den themselves, receiving a far less accommodating treatment. "They had not reached the bottom of the den," the Bible says, "before the lions overpowered them and crushed all their bones" (6:24).

King Darius then issued a new decree, commanding that all his people "tremble in fear before the God of Daniel,"

> "For he is the living God,
> and he endures forever;
> his kingdom will never be destroyed,
> and his dominion has no end.
> He rescues and delivers;
> he performs signs and wonders
> in the heavens and on the earth,
> for he has rescued Daniel
> from the power of the lions." (6:26–27)

That's not what the earth expected, but earth doesn't rule. Heaven rules.

That's the perspective from which we live, work, react, and pray.

SIMPLE, HUMBLE PRAYER

George Müller, who ran a network of orphanages in England for more than fifty years in the 1800s, famously never asked for a single donation, but prayed and trusted God entirely to provide for the work. He believed in Heaven's rule, even when every other sense said otherwise.

One often-told story about Müller's life and faith involves his being on board a ship, bound for America, when heavy fog descended on the open seas.[1] The captain had stayed awake for nearly a twenty-four-hour watch, slowing the vessel's speed to a crawl, with no end to the murky conditions in sight.

At some point, a tapping on his shoulder alerted the captain to a passenger in the steering room. "Captain, I have come to tell you that I must be in Quebec on Saturday afternoon."

That was not going to happen, the captain assured the concerned man. Could he not see what they were up against? No way would they be able to safely navigate the thickness of this fog in time to stay on their original schedule.

"Very well, if your ship can't take me, God will find some other means to take me. I have never broken an engagement in fifty-seven years."

The captain, turning dismissively back to his task, said he was sorry as sorry could be, but what was he expected to do?

"Let us go down to the chart room and pray," George Müller replied.

Preposterous. The captain, though a nominally practicing

Christian, told him he'd never heard of such a thing. "Mr. Müller, do you not know how dense the fog is?"

"No," he said, "my eye is not on the density of the fog, but on the living God, who controls every circumstance of my life." At that he got down on his knees and prayed what the captain remembered as one of the most basic, childlike prayers any grown man could utter. Touched by the sincerity of Müller's faith but unable to imagine how any prayer spoken so simply could arouse the Almighty, the captain stood for a silent moment, not sure what to make of this man.

"Captain," Müller said, breaking the awkward silence, "I have known my Lord for fifty-seven years, and there has never been a single day that I have failed to gain an audience with the King. Get up, Captain, and open the door, and you will find the fog is gone."

George Müller made his Saturday appointment.

Let's add, then, one final takeaway that's worth keeping before us when we think of how the prayers of God's people intersect with Heaven's rule. In both George Müller's and Daniel's prayers we see humility. Both of them kept a clear sense of who they were in relation to God. Both of them recognized the greatness and power of God. Both approached His throne with simple, humble faith.

Never mistake humble prayer for a lack of boldness. What it may not demonstrate in terms of volume and high-sounding language, it more than makes up for in unswerving confidence.

Daniel didn't take any glory or credit to himself for the

miracle that took place all that night and into the next morning. "My God sent his angel and shut the lions' mouths" (6:22). *"My God"*—the God who rules the heaven, the God who rules the seas, the God who rules in the direst, darkest, most dangerous places we can imagine. Perhaps you know these places all too well because you're in your own lions' den right now, and it is no child's story from a picture book.

Even if that is true, now is the time to pray. Now is the time to kneel and take your stand in the truth. Now is the time to refuse the worldly wisdom that says prayer is a waste of breath and time.

Every look around will make you think that might be right. But look up. Keep looking. Keep praying.

CHAPTER SEVEN

Battle Cry

*He is way too big for our finite minds to comprehend,
and yet his mercies are far too great
for him not to hear our cries for help.*

—*Pastor Bobby Scott*

MY FRIEND COLLEEN CHAO is a warrior. She was barely forty years old when her doctors discovered the menacing source behind some health issues she'd been encountering. After a lengthy battery of tests, they confirmed that an aggressive form of cancer was at work inside her body and that, in order to combat it, her treatment options would need to be equally extreme.

As I'm writing today, Colleen's cancer has reached stage 4 and has spread beyond its original site of discovery to her lymph nodes and bones—a cruel, staggering diagnosis. She is currently undergoing treatment with the goal of having a little more time on earth with her husband and their eleven-year-old son (who has also faced significant health challenges). It's possible that she could be in heaven by the time this book is released.

Colleen and her family have endured this unwanted trial

with remarkable faith and courage. Their testimony has been a true inspiration.[1] Yet not for an instant have they shied away from being real about this battle's grim features and the wracking pain and uncertainty it's interjected into their lives.

Shortly after receiving the most recent, dire prognosis of her metastasized breast cancer, Colleen sent out an email to her friends and family in which she reflected on the same Daniel that you and I have been learning to admire throughout the pages of this book. The Daniel who stood up to irascible opponents. The Daniel who faced down his own death sentence. The Daniel who spent a whole night in peace and quiet on the wrong side of a lion's cage.

But the book of Daniel, as perhaps you know, changes tone and direction as it transitions into the back half of his writing. Whereas the first six chapters are largely narrative and historical, the closing six chapters are taken up with visions, prophecies, and previews of distressing days yet to come, many of which are still awaiting their fulfillment in our own day or at some point in the near or distant future. In these chapters Daniel, now in his later years, speaks of frightening realities, of frontal assaults on God's chosen people. He never loses sight of the greatness of God, but neither does he downplay the real horrors that his people will yet face.

And the Daniel we see in these moments, though no less steadfast and resolved, also shows his human side. In her email, Colleen reminded us that the specter of coming disasters took a huge toll on Daniel, emotionally and physically:

- "My spirit was deeply distressed within me"
  (Dan. 7:15).
- "I, Daniel, was overcome and lay sick for days" (Dan.
  8:27).
- "No strength was left in me; my face grew deathly
  pale" (Dan. 10:8).
- "Anguish overwhelms me and I am powerless" (Dan.
  10:16).
- "There is no breath in me" (Dan. 10:17).

Perhaps you know the feeling. Colleen certainly does. And
in hearing of these same emotions in Daniel—some of the same
emotions that she, too, has been susceptible to feeling, often
without warning—she has felt surrounded and understood
in this fellowship of suffering. "I'm so grateful," she wrote in
her email, "that a mighty man of God like Daniel" could be
"wrecked by bad news, even while fully convinced of God's
abundant compassion."

In case you're speed-reading this chapter, you might want to
stop and read that last sentence again. This was the heart of the
matter for Daniel. And it's the heart of the matter for anyone
whose life is enveloped in the certainty that Heaven rules—a
reminder that we can be surrounded by wreckage on every side
and within while still affirming the unfailing love of God.

You see, trust in a good and great God and the presence of
overwhelming weakness are not mutually exclusive. These can
coexist without contradiction. Colleen's pain does not poke

holes in her testimony, even when it stabs so violently into her side, her back, her hip, her mind. In fact, she wrote, "a friend encouraged me early on to be okay with the consuming pain and grief, to be gentle with myself in the sleepless nights and the constant tears and the physical stress of it all." It's a word of advice she desperately needed to hear, a response she sees modeled in the example of Daniel.

"It's okay to be wrecked by bad news" of ensuing death and destruction—not in an ultimate sense, but in an immediate human sense. Because this life—let's just acknowledge it—is a battle. Life on this earth will always be a battle, and we humans will always be vulnerable to the pain of fighting it. But being wrecked by the battle is not the same as losing it.

We are ruled too well and loved too much to ever believe we are alone in our pain. And let's not forget that whatever "wrecking" we may experience in the here and now is not the end of the story, that it will not last forever. We are helped to endure this present pain with the assurance that all that is now wrecked will one day be redeemed.

In the first half of Daniel, the king is given dreams that Daniel interprets. In the second half of the book, Daniel is given four visions that an angel interprets. At times these visions read like an epic, high-fantasy novel—think *The Lord of the Rings*. To get a taste, read Daniel 7. How would you summarize the plot of this vision in a sentence or two?

BEASTLY PROBLEMS

In order to keep your biblical bearings when dealing with these visions of Daniel, begin by noticing that the one recorded in Daniel 7 occurred in "the first year of King Belshazzar" (v. 1) and the one from Daniel 8 "in the third year of King Belshazzar's reign" (v. 1). So we're backing up in time. These visions were given *before* that night in Daniel 5 when the mysterious hand appeared and wrote a message on the palace wall, and also before Daniel 6 when King Darius unwittingly set Daniel on a collision course with the lions' den.

More important, the scores of specific predictions in the visions of Daniel 7–12 were revealed to Daniel hundreds and even thousands of years before any of these ghastly events had actually taken place on the earth.

It's as if someone living in the mid-1600s had written a book describing in detail Germany's invasion of Poland at the start of World War II, the Jewish Holocaust, the Arab-Israeli War of 1948, the assassination of President John F. Kennedy, the Iran-Iraq war, the fall of the Berlin Wall, the Rwandan genocide, the worldwide pandemic of 2020, and many other such events that have yet to happen.

There's no way someone could do that, we'd say. Yet the visions in the second half of the book of Daniel speak of coming battles, coming rulers, coming calamities, and coming hope with a certainty that only God could know about.

God wanted Daniel—and believers of all eras—to get a glimpse of earth's happenings from heaven's perspective. He wanted us to see and understand that through all the rising and falling of kings and kingdoms on earth, Heaven continues to rule.

In Daniel's first vision, the one related in Daniel 7, he witnessed heaven's rule over the forces of nature: "Suddenly the four winds of heaven stirred up the great sea" (7:2). Those whirling winds symbolize great tumult and havoc coming on the earth.

Sounds familiar, doesn't it? Can't you feel that turmoil being stirred up around us today—in our homes, in our cities, in our world, churning like a cyclone? But make no mistake, this unsettling, this uprooting, this agitation, is a sign of Heaven at work.

The God of heaven is controlling the events of earth from above, working in and through the conflicts raging in our broken world, working despite our own frailties and brokenness, working every part and piece into a pattern that will one day take us home to Him through the storm. Yes, the waves are high, but we are not awash in the floating debris of fate. There is power and there is safety in Heaven's rule even when it hurts. Even when it's scary.

Daniel's first vision was definitely scary to him. For out of that turbulent sea came "four huge beasts" (7:3), one after the other.

- "The first was like a lion but had eagle's wings" (7:4)— then, as Daniel watched, its wings were ripped from its back, enabling the monster to stand to its feet and walk like a man.

- The second beast "looked like a bear" (7:5) except that it was weirdly imbalanced, "raised up on one side," and gorging itself on three fleshy ribs, rabidly gnawing them in its teeth.
- The third had the appearance of "a leopard" (7:6). It, too, was abnormally equipped with four wings, as well as having four distinct heads attached to its grisly body.
- Finally a fourth beast emerged—"incredibly strong, with large iron teeth" (7:7). And horns. Ten horns. Then it suddenly sprouted "another horn, a little one" (7:8), containing eyes and a mouth, through which it made sinister threats.

"The visions in my mind terrified me," Daniel admitted (7:15), causing him to plead for someone to shed light on why he had experienced these visions and what these hideous images meant.

These four beasts, he was told, represented "four kings who will rise from the earth" (7:17). Presumably these are the same kingdoms foreshadowed in Nebuchadnezzar's dream about the statue composed of various metals, revealed now with sharper graphics and in more haunting detail.

- The first beast appears to represent *Babylon.* Its transformation from animal form to more human qualities harks back to that season when Nebuchadnezzar lost his mind and was later restored to sanity.

- The second image contains markings of the *Medo-Persian empire,* which, as we have seen, took Babylon's place on the map. Out of its two unequal parts (Media and Persia), the one that eventually claimed dominance was Persia.
- The third, which along with the Medo-Persian beast reappears in different form in Daniel 8, is clearly a description of *Greece.* Alexander the Great routed the Persians in the mid-300s BC, but after his untimely death the resulting Greek empire was divided among his four leading generals—thus, the four heads.

The fourth beast, however, is less confined to the history books and more connected to our present and future. Keep in mind, though, that its fulfillment was entirely in the future when Daniel first saw it, and its implications would be realized, at least in part, in the increasingly dangerous battles God's people were soon to face.

Daniel immediately, intuitively, seemed to know this.

> "I wanted to be clear about the fourth beast, the one different from all the others, extremely terrifying, with iron teeth and bronze claws, devouring, crushing, and trampling with its feet whatever was left. I also wanted to know about the ten horns on its head and about the other horn that came up, before which three fell—the horn that had eyes, and a mouth that spoke arrogantly." (7:19–20)

"This horn," he said—the part of the vision that had distressed him more deeply than all the rest—"waged war against the holy ones and was prevailing over them" (7:21).

Now, commentators have varying opinions on the specific time frame and meaning of this mystery—of *all* these mysteries. But we do well, I think, to stay focused on what God has clearly revealed to us and on the way these ancient battles relate to the hostilities you and I face in our world today, as well as those that still await us going forward. And in it all we must remember that our God has never stopped and will never stop ruling over every nation, ruler, and event prefigured in these visions.

THE BATTLE WORSENS

What's the worst day you've ever lived through? What's the worst thing that ever happened to your family? What's the worst event in your nation's history? Of the many hard moments you've personally felt and witnessed, which event or which season has been the most challenging and painful?

The worst thing Daniel had ever experienced was Nebuchadnezzar's invasion of his homeland—the razing of the temple in Jerusalem and the exile of his people. In prayer he called this event "a disaster that is so great that nothing like what has been done to Jerusalem has ever been done under all of heaven" (Dan. 9:12). It seemed impossible that it could ever have happened. This land had been theirs since the days of Abraham, Isaac, and Jacob, and certainly since the days of Joshua, David, and

Solomon. Now it belonged to somebody else, and God's people belonged to Babylon. Daniel could not conceive of anything worse than that. But if their captivity and the demolishing of their temple qualified as being among the worst experiences in the history of his people, another atrocity was already on its way to join it, if not outrank it.

Back to the vision of the four beasts in Daniel 7. The "little horn" rising up on the fourth beast would obviously pose a major problem. And his "unwanted" poster is tacked up all over these visions that God handed down as a prophetic warning in the last half of Daniel.

So what—or who—does this powerful "little horn" represent? Hang in there with me. This gets a bit complicated—so much so that many people never read past Daniel 6, missing some of the most ominous threats and magnificent promises found anywhere in Scripture.

Following a worldwide conflict metaphorically described in Daniel 8 and following two hundred years of chronic warfare swirling around Israel, as described in Daniel 11—a Greek king by the name of Antiochus Epiphanes rose to power. He ruled from 175 BC until his death in 164 BC. And according to Daniel 11:21 he was a "despised" person. This word is also translated as "contemptible" (ESV), "despicable" (NASB), and "vile" (NKJV). I'm no Hebrew scholar, but here's what I take from all that: Antiochus Epiphanes was not a nice guy.

And his animosity toward the Jews led to the slaughter of thousands of them. But his assault, though physical, was also psychological and spiritual. Diabolical. Here's how this ruthless future ruler was described to Daniel and why what he heard caused him to be deeply distressed, even from his vantage point hundreds of years before the cruel despot's rise to power:

> "He will cause outrageous destruction
> and succeed in whatever he does.
> He will destroy the powerful
> along with the holy people.
> He will cause deceit to prosper
> through his cunning and by his influence,
> and in his own mind he will exalt himself.
> He will destroy many . . .
> he will even stand against the Prince of princes."
> (Dan. 8:24–25)

> "He will rage against the holy covenant and take action. On his return, he will favor those who abandon the holy covenant. His forces will rise up and desecrate the temple fortress. They will abolish the regular sacrifice and set up the abomination of desolation." (Dan. 11:30–31)

In 168 BC, nearly four hundred years after Daniel's vision of the four beasts, Antiochus Epiphanes did indeed invade Jerusalem, looting articles of property valued at more than a billion dollars in today's currency while taking into slavery whatever victims he didn't slaughter. He also ransacked the temple, which had been rebuilt with painstaking effort in the decades following the people's return. And perhaps most galling of all, he set up an idol of the Greek god Zeus in the place where the God of heaven was worshiped and offered a pig (the most unclean of offerings) as a sacrifice upon God's holy altar.

Maybe *despised* is not a bad enough word, after all.

You might wonder why there is so much emphasis in the book of Daniel on this vile, violent ruler. As the whole picture unfolds, we learn that he was an important character in the plot of the story God is writing in human history.

And, as it turns out, Antiochus and his atrocities, horrific as they were, will one day be outdone by yet another despicable ruler.

One of the things we learn in reading biblical prophecy is that it often contains both a *near* view and a *far* view. The near view, of course, can still be several centuries away, as in these visions concerning the renegade ruler. But much of the language God used in warning His people about Antiochus is also descriptive of another ruler who lurks in the far view, beyond Antiochus's reign of terror. A powerful false messiah will rise up in the end times to oppose God, persecute His people, and seek to control the world. We know him as the Antichrist.[2]

Here's how this demonically inspired oppressor is described in the New Testament:

> He opposes and exalts himself above every so-called god or object of worship, so that he sits in God's temple, proclaiming that he himself is God. (2 Thess. 2:4)

It began to speak blasphemies against God: to blaspheme his name and his dwelling—those who dwell in heaven. And it was permitted to wage war against the saints and to conquer them. (Rev. 13:6–7)

So, now these passages from Daniel hit closer to home, don't they? This is not just ancient history anymore. We haven't seen the last, maybe not really the first, certainly not yet the worst of this Antiochus-styled Antichrist. But his time is coming, perhaps much sooner than we realize. And even as we sit here today, with the end of time either near or far, we are targets of spiritual forces and rulers ("antichrists") who hate God and hate God's people, and whose way of attacking God is to attack God's people.

And even this we learn from Daniel.

The final vision given to Daniel is recorded in Daniel 10–12. It's a passage that is daunting to the most astute Bible students. But we know that all of God's Word is profitable for our instruction and growth, so I encourage you to persevere. Read chapter 10, asking God to give you insight. How would you describe what was happening on earth in this vision? What was happening in the unseen, heavenly realm? How was Daniel affected by what he saw? How did God encourage His servant?

The "great conflict" Daniel saw prophetically described in the vision in Daniel 10 (v. 1) would intensify for generations to come, against those who worshiped the God of Israel. But these battles on the ground, we discover, were actually visible expressions of a battle raging high above the earth. (Remember it's not enough to see things from *earth's* perspective. We need to also see all that is happening here on earth from *heaven's* perspective—and to trust that God knows and sees it all, even when much is hidden from our view.)

Daniel's dismay at these visions of uprisings and persecutions against his people burdened him so heavily that he lost himself in three long weeks of mournful prayer and fasting. Even then he received nothing he could call relief. He was as heartbroken three weeks later as he had been when he first experienced this revelation.

Then something happened. An angel appeared to him, bringing news of more battles and conflicts (see Daniel 11). But that hard news was prefaced by a heartening word:

> "From the first day that you purposed to understand and to humble yourself before your God, your prayers were heard. I have come because of your prayers." (10:12)

God had heard Daniel. God was listening. What wonderful assurance this must have brought to the distraught prophet.

But if his prayers had been heard and an answer sent three weeks ago, why the delay? Here's why: "The prince of the kingdom of Persia opposed me for twenty-one days," the angel reported. The conflict might have gone on longer, except that "Michael, one of the chief princes, came to help me" (10:13). In other words, there was more to what was happening than what Daniel could see with his eyes.

Commentators agree that the "prince of the kingdom of Persia" was not a human ruler like those Daniel had served throughout his lifetime. The angel was referring to a high-ranking spiritual being who wielded power and influence over the Persian empire. This seems to suggest that there are powerful demons—fallen angels, messengers of Satan—who are connected to world empires, rulers, and governments. They work in unseen ways behind many visible political and cultural developments and are always attempting to sabotage God's rule and harm His people.

The battles taking place around us on earth reflect a greater spiritual conflict taking place in the heavens. The battles we observe in our world between good and evil, between truth and lies, or between the people of God and those who oppose God reflect something of this otherworldly warfare. So do the battles that rage within our families, within our churches, within the cells of our bodies, or anywhere else in our lives or our world.

"Our struggle," says Paul the apostle, "is not against flesh and blood, but against the rulers, against the authorities, against the cosmic powers of this darkness, against evil, spiritual forces in the heavens" (Eph. 6:12). This is not just the Bible talking Bible-y things. This is God's Word opening our eyes to realities more real than our real-world things.

We do not live merely in a 3D world, where everything we see happening around us is simply the cause-and-effect result of people interacting with people, of purely natural processes that occasionally catch us in the crossfire. We live here on earth amid the clashing and clanging of a conflict taking place in the unseen heavenly dimension. And at times the enemies of God and His people seem to be winning. In fact, Daniel is told directly of a terrible time when many of God's people "will fall by the sword and flame, and they will be captured and plundered" (Dan. 11:33).

It happened in the centuries after Daniel saw this vision, it has happened again and again since then, and it still happens today. In such seasons it sometimes appears that God is powerless to stop the opposition or to help His people. But that's simply not true. All of this is under His control, and, importantly, only "for a time" (11:33).

This evil spirit over Persia had tried to hinder the angelic messenger from bringing Daniel the answer to his prayers. And that evil spirit succeeded for a period of time—until God said, "Time's up" and sent one of His chief angels, Michael, to help the messenger angel, who was finally able to make his way to Daniel's side.

The forces of evil are strong. They are capable of creating hurdles, difficulties, and delays for God's people. But be sure of this: they can only oppose; they cannot prevail. They are under Heaven's rule, and they cannot stop His work from being accomplished.

At the end of the day, whatever trouble they can cause has already been defeated by the plans and purposes of God in Christ to transform evil's curse into blessing for all the redeemed.

Even as we battle on.

WHEN THINGS LOOK BAD

Mark and Michelle Leach are related to my husband by marriage. Their second child, a daughter they named Blair, was born with a rare genetic mutation that caused severe physical and cognitive disabilities and severely impacted just about every bodily function. The first two years of her life have been spent cycling in and out of the hospital, including undergoing open-heart sur-gery at two months of age. As you might imagine, life with Blair has been a far cry from the life that any parent expects when they find out they're expecting.

The couple had told God twenty weeks into this pregnancy—when the first clues of Blair's condition presented themselves, with their other daughter not yet a year old—that the one thing they could not handle was a child with acute, long-term needs. They prayed that the scans and samples were mistaken, that the worst-case scenarios were only being presented to them as a way of providing perspective, of balancing their outlook, desperately hoping that the end result surely wouldn't be as critical as they were being told it could potentially be.

As soon as Blair was born, however, the first look at her face told them otherwise. Despite all their questioning and all their pleading, despite the genuine sincerity of all their praying, God's answer to their cries appeared shut up in the heavenly realm, unheeded. This was bad and unlikely to get better.

It didn't.

Following a month of intensive-care heroics, the hospital sent them home with a supply of tubes and wires and com-plicated medical equipment to begin caring 24-7 for a new daughter they loved with all their heart but truly didn't know how to care for.

Mark and Michelle transparently acknowledge that "Life with Blair is really hard. By worldly standards, she gives little in return."[3] Most days come with more questions than answers, with fatigue that barely earns a moment's reprieve, with nerves worn thin, and with God's silence making them feel sometimes as if He doesn't want to be bothered by their problems.

It's an everyday, seemingly unending battle—physically, spiritually, all of it. "We wrestled with the Lord," they admit, "begging Him to heal Blair and give us a daughter free of challenges. And His answer was no. But His answer was no in order to give us something much, much greater." New depths of compassion in their hearts. Truer perspectives on their roles as parents of God's gifts. Opportunities to testify about His faithful provision.

And more of Himself than they'd ever experienced before. Michelle says,

> I feel the Lord's protection from thoughts that wander down the road of unknown days ahead. He places hedges around me when I feel the temptation to compare Blair with other children. By His grace alone I feel freedom from a life ruled by comparison, anxiety, and fear.

Though painful—oh, so painful—Mark and Michelle are coming to see that God's "no" answer is not callous or random but is actually part of His good plan for their lives. That their God is winning a hard-fought battle, without a thing the enemy can do about it. Michelle shares that peace came as she began to realize

> God was on a mission of grace to use Blair to make me into a woman who better resembles the image of Jesus. Like gold that's put through fire, He is already using Blair

to burn away the sin that displeased Him in order to refine me.

Here, though, is the one statement from this young couple that most gripped me, not only in terms of how Heaven's rule can carry us through our battles, but also in terms of the way the Lord uses those battles to shape grieving parents like Mark and Michelle—and people like us, in the throes of trials where we feel at or beyond the breaking point:

> He is using Blair to help adjust our focus on that which is eternal and fix our gaze heavenward, in order that these short years here on earth are kept in their proper place compared to an eternity with Jesus.

This word, like Colleen Chao's word, sounds so much to me like Daniel.

Their battles look so terrifying, their burdens feel so unbearable. Yet their eyes keep looking up.

KEEP WATCHING

One of the things you almost can't keep from noticing across this tapestry of visions recorded in the book of Daniel is how consistently he maintained a posture of "watching." You might want to highlight these references in your Bible, as I've done in mine. For example: "I was watching" (Dan. 7:2), "while I was watching" (7:6), "while I was watching" (7:7) . . .

Even when feeling exhausted and overwhelmed by the battles taking place around him and those yet to come, Daniel remained spiritually alert, the eyes of his heart wide open and lifted upward.

We are prone to limit our sights to earthly realities—watching the news on an endless loop, watching how our mate or our kids or our boss are acting. We draw conclusions and determine how to react on the basis what we can see down here. But Daniel watched for what *God* was doing in the midst of, over and above, all the political intrigue and chaos going on around him on earth. That is what kept his heart and mind calm and gave him an excellent spirit and the wisdom to know what to do.

Watching for the right things, looking in the right direction, will give us courage and comfort in the swirl of whatever may be happening around us. It is key to remaining steady over the long haul, to not being stirred up by earthly strife, earthly threats, earthly pressures, and earthly people. It is key to our continuing to serve the Lord when times are stormy, confusing, depraved, and godless.

But it's not just a matter of watching. Jesus told His disciples to "watch and pray" (Matt. 26:41 ESV). And that's exactly what Daniel did.

And we're not just talking about occasional, quick, distracted glances in God's direction. Watching was an ongoing, established way of life for Daniel: "as I kept watching" (Dan. 7:9), "I continued watching" (7:13).

When it doesn't look like God is doing anything in our

situation or our world, we're tempted to give up watching for Him and His activity. I believe this is one reason why so many Christians are chronically anxious and discouraged—because they've stopped watching. Or because their attention is fixed on what's happening down here on earth, but they've forgotten to lift up their eyes to heaven.

So don't stop watching. Don't stop looking for what God is doing. And keep watching the right things. Keep your eyes in God's Word. Observe what plans He is unfolding here on earth. And always, always keep your eyes on Christ, the risen Lord of all creation.

One day after his three weeks of fervent prayer (Dan. 10:2–3), Daniel was standing among a group of people on the banks of the Tigris River when he instinctively "looked up" (vv. 4–5), still much in mind of all the things that had been worrying him throughout his long, intense season of spiritual wrestling.

Now look what he saw when he looked up. Look at *Who* he saw:

> . . . a man dressed in linen, with a belt of gold from Uphaz around his waist. His body was like beryl, his face like the brilliance of lightning, his eyes like flaming torches, his arms and feet like the gleam of polished bronze, and the sound of his words like the sound of a multitude. (10:5–6)

If this description sounds familiar to you, that's no accident.

Compare it to the description John gave of the figure who spoke to him in a heavenly vision in the first chapter of Revelation:

> . . . one like the Son of Man, dressed in a robe and with a golden sash wrapped around his chest. The hair of his head was white as wool—white as snow—and his eyes like a fiery flame. His feet were like fine bronze as it is fired in a furnace, and his voice like the sound of cascading waters. (Rev. 1:13–15)

Nearly identical, right? That's because the vision Daniel saw, which nobody else around him could see (maybe because they weren't looking up?) is another Christophany, or Old Testament visitation of Christ. Here in plain view was the Son of God, the promised Messiah, who would one day come to earth as a man to redeem this fallen world, visiting Daniel in his distress.

Answering Daniel's pain and his prayers with His presence. And telling us something we need to know about our own place in the battles that surround us.

We think we're just praying. Just sitting here with our hands folded by our bedside or with our books spread out before us on the kitchen table. Sensing we're situated in the middle of a battle that is bigger than we are. Wondering why we're not seeing or hearing anything from heaven. If maybe we're not saying it right, or if God is simply too far away to hear us. Wondering why the answers we long for are not coming.

Daniel thought he was just praying too. He'd been praying

all his life, and for three whole weeks he'd been praying more intensely than ever before. But he was just beginning to comprehend the kind of warfare he was engaging in from his knees—the battles being fought; the kingdoms in conflict down here on the terrestrial globe and far above, in unseen spiritual dimensions; the earthly sovereigns who thought they were in charge and even more powerful, unseen demonic and angelic beings, the past and the future. And above it all, unquestionably victorious, was the Most High God. Daniel had never seen his God like this, radiating such visible brilliance and glory—more awe-inspiring than any beastly opponent, no matter how intolerable or terrifying.

It's the lesson of looking up, always watching, always praying.[4] The battle is real, but Heaven rules. And in ways we cannot fathom, our prayers down here, frail and small as we are, have a part to play in His grand plan.

> The battle is real, but Heaven rules. And in ways we cannot fathom, our prayers down here, frail and small as we are, have a part to play in His grand plan.

THREE WATCHWORDS FOR THE BATTLE

As I scan these four visions in the last half of Daniel, I see a number of things God communicated to him while Daniel watched, while Daniel was looking up. These three watchwords, spoken over the din of continual raging battles here on earth, infused

Daniel with courage and comfort in the thick of all the chaos and the brandishing of enemy arms. They will do the same for you and for me if we receive them.

HR WATCHWORD #1: "I will tell you the truth."

We've all got our feelings. We've all got our wants and wishes for how we'd like our lives to go. But as with Mark and Michelle, the battle is often what motivates us to look up, in the midst of surroundings so much more difficult than how we'd ever imagined possible, and to see the truth in a way we might never have taken time to notice it otherwise. To see the truth and be changed by it. Captured by it. Inspired by it. Blessed by it.

Satan, the determined enemy of God and His people, is a mastermind of lies. He lies, his demons lie, and so do the people and institutions through which they work on the earth. Lies are everywhere around us—powerful, pervasive, as if to communicate by the sheer weight and reach of their arguments that God's eternal rule is up for grabs, that surely there's more truth in what the world says, through all its pride, entitlement, and comparison, than in what God says. Insisting that "your truth" is what really matters.

But the angel told Daniel, "I will tell you the truth" (Dan. 11:2). And we too have God's Word of truth, which sustains us, supports us, strengthens us, secures us. Truth is our superpower, our weapon in battle: "the sword of the Spirit—which is the word of God" (Eph. 6:17). In sports terms, it's what we use to play *defense* as well as *offense.*

Yes, sometimes we are exhausted from the battle and, yes, sometimes we hurt so deeply. But then we look up and see that Man clothed in linen, and we recalibrate our lives according to His truth, as revealed to us in living Scripture and daily enlivened for us by the indwelling Holy Spirit. And somehow, in that truth, we find the strength to keep on fighting.

HR WATCHWORD #2: **"Peace to you, be very strong."**

"Now I have no strength," Daniel said, "and there is no breath in me" (Dan. 10:17). He reached a point where there was no more fight in him. Yet the Lord sent help to him—the angel's touch, and the angel's words of encouragement: "Peace to you; be very strong" (10:19).

Most of us don't talk about angels a lot in our daily lives, with our Western mindset so conditioned toward what is natural, visible, and explainable. But the Bible makes it clear that angels are real—"ministering spirits sent out to serve those who are going to inherit salvation" (Heb. 1:14). These servants of God are among the many means He has of getting His peace and strength through to us.

So never despair of looking up for help, even at your most weak and breathless. "Heaven rules" does not mean God is an impersonal, uncaring, unresponsive potentate, detached from our very real concerns and crises. Though He is sovereign and mighty, though He is glorious beyond compare, the Lord hears and responds to the prayers of His people and gives both peace and strength.

As a mother is drawn toward the cries of her helpless, tiny baby, our great God is moved to bring comfort and supply to us at the sound of our prayers, as they are poured out in the midst of the fiercest battle. Those prayers are the "battle cry" that Heaven loves to hear; they move our King to send supernatural reinforcements to engage with us in the fray.

HR WATCHWORD #3: **"You are treasured by God."**

I hope this wasn't news to Daniel. I hope it's not news to you.

"At the beginning of your petitions an answer went out," the angel said to him, "and I have come to give it"—why?—"for you are treasured by God" (Dan. 9:23). Not once, but three times, Daniel received this same assurance from the angel (see 10:11, 19). Apparently Daniel needed to be reminded—as do you and I.

God from ancient times said He chose Israel "to be a people for his treasured possession" (Deut. 14:2 ESV). The people of God are treasured by God. He loves them. And whether you feel it to be true or not, He loves you. He hears you and answers your prayers.

You and I are put through so many challenges in the course of our lives. We're forced to endure all kinds of demeaning, humiliating pressure from the battles of this world. But look up and remember who you are. Scripture says of Jesus that He was "rejected by men but in the sight of God chosen and precious" (1 Peter 2:4 ESV). You may be rejected by the elites and the scoffers of this world. But if you are in Christ, in the sight of God, you are "chosen and precious." God says to His own, *I love you. I hear you. I know you. I've got you.*

Even within the nerve-bending, never-ending presence of such titanic conflict, God wants you repeatedly reminded that you are precious to Him, that He is tenderly mindful of you. That you are treasured by Him.

> Stay tethered to the truth. Be strong and be at peace. You are treasured by God.

"So our family has taken a walk in Daniel's shoes," my friend Colleen wrote, in wrapping up her email update.

> We've cried out in grief. We've banked on God's compassion and faithfulness. We've felt overcome, physically sick, and emotionally weary beyond anything we've ever known. We've also keenly sensed that we are "treasured by God," even in the midst of the grief.

She closed with these words:

> God may entrust me, and you, with devastating news. But when we are treasured by God, we have all of His infinite resources at our fingertips. Peace is ours even as we quake. Strength is ours even in great weakness.

That's the message from both Colleen and Daniel that I hope you will take to heart.

Stay tethered to the truth.
Be strong and be at peace.
You are treasured by God.
Battle on.

CHAPTER EIGHT

The Long View

Someday this upside-down world
will be turned right side up.
Nothing in all eternity will turn it back again.

—Randy Alcorn

IN THE SPRING OF 2020, when the first COVID lockdowns were beginning to take effect (remember that?), a lot of famous and not-so-famous people turned to social media to communicate with the outside world. One of them was actress Gal Gadot, best known as the star of the movie *Wonder Woman.* Along with a who's-who slate of her celebrity friends, Gadot created a YouTube video intended to lift the spirits of those brought low by the fears and uncertainties of the days ahead. With selfie cameras capturing each personality's face one by one in scenes from their homes and yards and closets and patios, the video pieced together a line-by-line singing of the John Lennon one-world-peace anthem "Imagine."[1]

You know that song, don't you? Since it first appeared in 1971 it's been hard to miss. But have you ever really listened to the lyrics? Lennon's song asks us to envision a world in which there's no afterlife—no heaven to be gained, no hell to be avoided. Nothing to live for but today. What we can see, hear, touch, and experience in the here and now—that's all there is.

Gadot's rendition of this rock classic got me to thinking about the implications of such a world, if it were possible. How could it bring hope and comfort to someone in the midst of crisis to imagine there's no heaven above (and, by implication, no God)? How could that possibly lift anyone's spirits or provide hope?

To me, the very idea of such of world is a complete downer. And I don't think I'm alone, judging from the pandemic of anxiety and depression engulfing us today. If there's really no heaven—or if Heaven is impotent to do anything about what is happening on earth—if anyone or anything other than God in heaven rules . . . we truly have no hope, no comfort.

Faced with evil and pain, we are forced to rely on our own wisdom, our own strength, our own strategies. We are left alone, helpless against the floods that overwhelm us.

But thanks be to God (yes, there *is* a God in heaven above), there's a far better option. And it's not a figment of our imagination. It's true.

Over the past several months, I've been meditating on another lyric. I recite it often—as I pillow my head at night, when I waken during the night, before my feet hit the floor in the morning, sometimes as I'm doing my hair or cooking dinner or driving to run an errand. These words, now stitched into the fabric of my heart, have brought me great encouragement and peace. They have given me courage and strength.

They come from the Heidelberg Catechism, a teaching document first published in 1563. Arranged in the typical question-and-answer format used for training believers and their children in the foundations of Christian faith, the catechism begins by asking: "What is your only comfort in life and in death?"

Think of it: more than four hundred fifty years ago, people were looking for comfort, just as they are today. All of us seek comfort when confronted with the challenges of living and the prospect of death—not just literal death, but the death of dreams, hopes, security, plans, relationships, and more.

So how would you answer that question? Where do you turn for comfort and hope when the world feels out of control, when your life doesn't turn out at all as you'd hoped? Your answer matters.

Here's the response found in the Heidelberg Catechism. These ancient words are worth reading (and rereading) slowly.

Q. What is your only comfort in life and in death?

A. That I am not my own,
but belong—
body and soul,
in life and in death—
to my faithful Savior, Jesus Christ.

He has fully paid for all my sins with his precious blood,
and has set me free from the tyranny of the devil.
He also watches over me in such a way
that not a hair can fall from my head
without the will of my Father in heaven;
in fact, all things must work together for my salvation.

Because I belong to him,
Christ, by his Holy Spirit,
assures me of eternal life
and makes me wholeheartedly willing and ready
from now on to live for him. [2]

Our only comfort in life and in death? There is a God. He rules from heaven. And because He does, we are free from guilt and shame over our past; our present circumstances are being perfectly ordained and orchestrated by Him; and our future is bright with hope.

We can be at peace. Everything is under control. Forever.

Imagine that.

WHAT TO EXPECT

Hardly a day passes that I am not in touch with someone (or someones) who are going through really hard things. In some cases these trials just seem to go on and on and on, with no end in sight. Several recent examples come to mind:

- a friend who has had to move out of her beautiful home after years of chronic, severe illness that rendered her husband unable to work, required her to become a full-time caregiver, and wrecked them financially (She texted me, "We're officially homeless.")
- a couple who have spent years caring for two sets of elderly parents with dementia and significant health issues
- a middle-aged single woman who had to leave her career decades ago to devote herself to the care of her elderly, widowed mother
- a single woman who has always yearned to have a family to love and serve, though she is now past childbearing years
- a man in the midst of a messy, drawn-out lawsuit related to a fatal accident that took place on a piece of property he owns
- a couple with two adult children who are breaking their hearts with foolish, destructive choices
- a woman whose husband announced a dozen years ago that he was no longer a Christian, abruptly stopped going to church with her, and has no interest in anything of a spiritual nature—without really a reason except to say that "they're all hypocrites there" (This wife has stayed with her husband. She loves him. And she's HR enough to accept the call of living out her

faith at home in a way that she hopes will woo him back to Jesus. But she can't help wondering how much longer it will be like this.)

The common denominator in each of these situations? Prolonged troubles with no evident solution or hope of change. Faced with pain and problems that seem interminable, all of these people have wrestled with the same questions. Perhaps you have as well:

- How long will this last? (whatever *this* is)
- How is it going to turn out? (whatever *it* is)

It's not wrong to ask these questions and to wish we knew the answers. Daniel at eighty-plus years, when he thought back on the trials he'd endured throughout his life and then received these messages from God about the persecution and oppression still to come against his people in the future, was faced with the same questions:

- "How long until the end of these . . . things?" (Dan. 12:6)
- "What will be the outcome of these things?" (12:8)

We *want* to know how much longer. We feel like we *need* to know how it will it end. *Where is this going? What will life look like for me a year from now, five years from now, ten years from now? Will I even be here?* It would make all the difference in the world, we think, if we could only know. It would make a difference in how we live now.

We're tired of imagining.

Imagining doesn't help. But HR does.

"Heaven rules" is a huge part of the answer to everything.

It's not an easy answer. It's not a make-it-all-better answer. It may not seem like nearly specific enough of an answer to the painful questions you've been asking and their impact on your life and your family.

But imagine if God had no answer to give. Imagine if Heaven didn't rule. Imagine if no one was working above and inside our questions, working in advance and in response to our prayers—One who not only knows where everything is going but is actively taking it there and will be delivering it right on time. In His own time. At the perfect time. One who knows us and loves us and is making us part of this grand story He is writing.

> Imagining doesn't help. But HR does. "Heaven rules" is a huge part of the answer to everything.

But we really don't have to imagine what life would be like without "Heaven rules." Because Heaven *does* rule, even when we don't understand what is happening around us and to us.

Daniel wanted to understand. Again and again he entreated Heaven and Heaven's messengers to help him understand.

> "I approached one of those who were standing by and asked him to clarify all this." (Dan. 7:16)

"I wanted to be clear. . . . wanted to know." (7:19–20)

"I, Daniel, was watching the vision and trying to understand it." (8:15)

"I was greatly disturbed . . . and could not understand." (8:27)

And the Lord, far from being annoyed by or indifferent to these pleas, not only responded to Daniel's desire for understanding but often offered at least a partial explanation through His angelic messengers:

"Gabriel, explain the vision to this man." (8:16)

"I am here to tell you what will happen." (8:19)

"Daniel, I've come now to give you understanding." (9:22)

"I have come to help you understand." (10:14)

So it's not that God is bothered by these questions or is unwilling to answer them. He knows why we ask. But He also knows what we need to know, and He has given us His Word and His Spirit so that we are not left clueless. He liberally gives us what we need even when He is withholding what we don't, knowing that if He were an open search engine, His answers would only lead to more questions, diminish our need for faith, and actually heighten our fears and unsettledness.

God possesses knowledge about us and about how He chooses to govern us and our world which, for our own good, is "secret and sealed until the time of the end" (Dan. 12:9)—secret except to tell us that we are being "purified, cleansed, and refined" (12:10) through each day's living out of all these unknowns. The waiting is how He is preparing us—we, His "holy ones"—to "receive the kingdom and possess it forever, yes, forever and ever" (7:18).

In other words, when He says, "I know something you don't know," He doesn't say it with a smug shake of His head, but with a fatherly wink of "just you wait" excitement. And while we wait—as hard as waiting can be—we can be confident that *He* knows how long our circumstance will last, and *He* knows how it's going to turn out.

Truth is, it's going to turn out even better than we imagine.

THE ULTIMATE SUCCESS STORY

In looking at this second half of Daniel, my intent has been to stay at a thirty-thousand-foot level. There's a lot we can't know, or can only speculate at knowing, by taking the plane much lower. But even from high altitude, without trying to pin name tags on each of the bad actors who play a role in these prophecies, God provides us with several key landmarks that could hardly be any clearer.

Here are four important reminders that have been steadying to my own heart as I've marinated in the latter portion of the book of Daniel.

Read Daniel 7 once again. What do you find in this passage that can encourage you in the midst of any hard circumstances in your life (or that of someone you know) for which there seem to be no end? Now keep your Bible nearby as we fly back over this patchwork of ground—these prophetic pictures that frightened Daniel so much initially—and look for details we might not have noticed the first time. Let's see if the pressure of our own battles and the pervasiveness of all this conflict in the world might just have been obscuring the answers God has already given for our comfort and courage.

HR REMINDER #1: **There's an end.**

Look again at that fourth beast from Daniel 7, the one with the horns, the teeth, the claws, and the arrogant voice of defiance, the one who "waged war against the holy ones and was prevailing over them" (7:21). Okay, that last description is true. That horrible beast was "prevailing over" God's people—dominating them, defeating them, *until* . . . Daniel 7:22 says clearly that this happened only "*until* the Ancient of Days arrived and a judgment was given in favor of the holy ones of the Most High."

How I love that word *until*. What it represents gives me goose bumps at times. I think of you and me and our many tiring battles, but also of the places in this world where God's "holy ones" are being openly badgered and persecuted, shamefully treated because of unjust, ungodly rulers.

How long will this go on? *Until.*

There's an "until" to every one of our losses, pains, and grievances. All these terrors and atrocities have permission to last *until* "the court will convene, and his dominion [that of the enemy who oppresses us] will be taken away, to be completely destroyed forever" (7:26).

Did you hear that? Yes, one day the Ancient of Days will hold court, and the righteous Judge of all the earth will hand down the verdict—"Guilty!"—to every cruel, arrogant, antichrist ruler, to every

> ∧
>
> How long will this go on? *Until.* There's an "until" to every one of our losses, pains, and grievances.
>
> ∨

instigator of every conflict. Their power will come to an end, and we will begin to reign with Christ forever.

In the meantime, of course, "there will be war" (Dan. 9:26). In fact, one of these warmongers, the book of Daniel says, "will destroy the city and the sanctuary" (9:26)—a prophecy that in the near view was fulfilled when Jerusalem and its temple were destroyed again in AD 70 by the Romans. In the far view it speaks of the destructive activity of the Antichrist, who is still to come near the end of the age. And in between the near and the far views, God's enemies relentlessly spew out their venom against His holy ones.

But the violence and sacrilege wreaked by these adversaries will only continue

> *"until* the decreed destruction
> is poured out on the desolator." (9:27)

It's decreed. The destruction and desolation these evildoers have poured out on others will one day be poured out on them. They will be no more.

HR REMINDER #2: **There's a time.**

Heaven doesn't rule only in a general sense. The end of evil's dominion is not something that, while certain in theory, is still being hammered out in committee when it comes to the exact timing of when things will actually happen. No. The end is not just near; the end is fixed. It is already on the calendar. In ink. In blood. The clock is ticking, and the numbers that are running down on the timer have already been locked in.

To get a clearer sense of this point, skim through the book of Daniel and highlight each appearance of the words *time* or *times*.

One of the things that often sticks in people's minds when they think of the last several chapters in Daniel is that these prophecies include a number of specific, if cryptic, time frames. The angel who spoke to Daniel in chapter 9, for instance, said,

> "Seventy weeks are decreed
> about your people and your holy city." (9:24)

This span of seventy weeks is further broken down into "seven weeks" plus "sixty-two weeks" (9:25) plus another "one week," and there's even mention of something that will happen "in the middle of the week" (9:27).

What in the world does all of that mean? And what about those references to "a time, times, and half a time" (Dan. 7:25; 12:7)?

So much of this seems perplexing and mind-numbing to us. But here's what's clear: in God's mind the program is already determined and carefully timed.

I can't tell you what every bit of this chronology entails because I simply don't know. No human does, with certainty. But the fact that

> The end is not just near; the end is fixed. It is already on the calendar. The clock is ticking, and the numbers that are running down on the timer have already been locked in.

math is utilized as a teaching device in these descriptions tells us all we really need to know. God, who is the ultimate mathematician, has an exact answer to our "how long" questions. All the coordinates are in place. All the lines and arcs and parabolas are drawn. Your battle and mine end . . . *right there!* His finger has already pinpointed the precise spot.

So when the Scripture says, "the time had come" (Dan. 7:22) for the Judge to rule and His people to be vindicated, it's talking about God's perfect time, His established time, His "appointed time"—a phrase that appears throughout these prophecies (see Dan. 8:19; 11:27, 29, 35).

Our enemy will be able to notch successes against us for a time. How long? "Until the time of wrath is completed" (11:36). In other words, you and I and all the rest of God's people will keep facing struggles and opposition as we journey through life, perhaps even up to and including our deaths. But God's promise is that we will be "refined, purified, and cleansed" through those ordeals (11:35).[3] And nothing can keep our deliverance and the demise of every enemy from coming "at the appointed time" (11:35).

Done deal. Final buzzer. God controls the game clock. And at the very instant when it winds down to all zeroes, our waiting for answers will all be over.

HR REMINDER #3: **There's a winner.**

I don't think it is any coincidence that the first beast in Daniel's first vision was "like a lion" (Dan. 7:4). I wonder if, years later, one of the reasons he didn't fear the lions' den the way he might otherwise have done is because he'd seen a lion already—and a bear, and a leopard, and whatever carnivore the fourth beast was supposed to be—and had seen them all meet their immortal match one night while he was lying in bed, watching.

> "Thrones were set in place,
> and the Ancient of Days took his seat.
> His clothing was white like snow,
> and the hair of his head like whitest wool.
> His throne was flaming fire;
> its wheels were blazing fire.
> A river of fire was flowing,
> coming out from his presence.

Thousands upon thousands served him;
ten thousand times ten thousand stood before him.
The court was convened,
and the books were opened." (7:9–10)

Daniel was looking into heaven (as you and I can get glimpses of heaven through descriptions like this one and others that God has given us in His Word). And around God's throne in heaven he saw fire. Flaming fire. Blazing fire. A river of fire. Everywhere fire.

Fire is a symbol of intense purity. God's fire is what purifies us so that we—as unholy and impure as we are—can be made to stand in His presence and not be obliterated. We need His fire. We need His cleansing and refining because nothing—and no one—corrupted, tainted, or impure can survive in the presence of holy God.

Seated on a throne in the midst of that fire, utterly unconsumed by the blaze, sat the eternal, sovereign Ruler of the universe, the supreme Judge of the Supreme Court of heaven. Myriads of angelic hosts attended Him, ready to carry out His will and execute His righteous judgment on the earth.

That's the heavenly view. But let's follow Daniel's eyes back down to earth, after having seen God's power on such awesome display. And let's bring the rule of God's kingdom down into our own viewfinder as we look around and are distressed by the haughtiness of human leaders in our day. Keep watching as Daniel did:

"I watched, then, because of the sound of the arrogant words the horn was speaking. As I continued watching, the beast was killed and its body destroyed and given over to the burning fire." (7:11)

Winner, winner, beasts for dinner. These beasts, our beasts, have "a certain period of time" (7:12). We don't know how long it may be. Only God knows. But we can be certain their time is limited, their defeat sure, and that our God is seeing to their destruction. Personally. Through His Son.

Daniel saw this, too, as he watched:

"Suddenly one like a son of man
was coming with the clouds of heaven.
He approached the Ancient of Days
and was escorted before him.
He was given dominion
and glory and a kingdom,
so that those of every people,
nation, and language
should serve him.
His dominion is an everlasting dominion
that will not pass away,
and his kingdom is one
that will not be destroyed." (7:13–14)

What a rousing reminder that hell may raise its back, but Heaven rules—and will rule forever.

But that brings us back to the "how long" question. How long will we have to wait for all this to happen? How long before evil is defeated and all creation bows and acknowledges God as the undisputed King of the universe?

A well-known spiritual affirms that it will be soon:

> Soon-a will be done-a with the troubles of the world. . . .
> No more weeping and a-wailing. . . .
> I'm goin' to live with God. [4]

But when is "soon"? How long till we're done with the troubles of this world? How long till weeping and wailing are no more?

Even the angels want to know that. We hear one of them in Daniel 8 ask,

> "How long will the events of this vision last—the regular sacrifice, the rebellion that makes desolate, and the giving over of the sanctuary and of the army to be trampled?" (v. 13).

Fair question. Is there an answer?

Yes, and it's circled on God's calendar: "For 2,300 evenings and mornings; then the sanctuary will be restored" (8:14).

I'm not sure when that will be. Neither are you. But here's what we do know: God has this timed down to the hour. And when that moment comes, our enemy will be no longer. "He will be broken," though "not by human hands" (8:25). The same stone that broke away from the mountain and crushed Nebuchadnezzar's statue to dust—"without a hand touching it" (Dan. 2:45)—will crush every foe, end every battle, silence every accuser.

"Completely destroyed forever" (Dan. 7:26).

And then

> "the kingdom, dominion, and greatness of the kingdoms under all of heaven will be given to the people, the holy ones of the Most High. His kingdom will be an everlasting kingdom, and all rulers will serve and obey him." (7:27)

There's a clear winner in the ring. All rulers will lay down their arms and bow before the King of heaven. And we get to win with Him, because . . .

HR REMINDER #4: **There's a Savior.**

Why do you think God preserved stories in the Bible like that of Shadrach, Meshach, and Abednego and their deliverance from the fiery furnace? Or like Daniel and his deliverance from the lions' den? Did He do it to leave the impression that He will always rush into any problem we face and whisk us out of it so that we're left untouched?

I don't think your life experiences and mine would bear that out. We do live under God's roof and His rule, but trouble can surely get through the door. And sometimes, it seems, it comes to stay, no matter how fervently we pray for deliverance.

But the deliverance we need most—as a right-sized view of

God makes clear to us—is to be rescued from God's righteous wrath for our sin. That's the fiery furnace, the mouth of the hungry lion, that not even death can enable us to escape. And that judgment is something we all deserve.

But God in His goodness, mercy, and grace—God, who alone has the right and rule to do it—has given us a Deliverer: Jesus Christ. And these stories in Daniel, written many years before the appearance of Jesus on earth, point us toward this good news of the gospel, apart from which none of us can ever be saved.

"We have sinned," Daniel prayed in chapter 9 on behalf of himself and his people. We have "done wrong." We have "acted wickedly" and "rebelled" against what God has commanded us (Dan. 9:5). "We have not listened" (9:6); we have not followed "his instructions that he set before us" (9:10). We have "broken your law and turned away, refusing to obey you" (9:11). "We have not sought the favor of the LORD our God by turning from our iniquities and paying attention to your truth" (9:13).

Daniel never shied away from an honest appraisal of his own sinfulness and that of his people. He knew all too well what they deserved. But still he pleaded with God to be merciful, to "listen and act" in their behalf, to provide a way out.

God did listen. And He promised to act. While Daniel was still praying and pouring out his heart to God, the Lord sent His messenger Gabriel to give Daniel "understanding" (Dan. 9:22) of His unfolding redemptive plan:

"Seventy weeks are decreed. . .
to bring the rebellion to an end,
to put a stop to sin,
to atone for iniquity,
to bring in everlasting righteousness." (9:24)

The angel also spoke of an "Anointed One" who would rule for a time and then be "cut off" (9:26) after "seven weeks and sixty-two weeks" (9:25). Bible scholars mostly agree that the "weeks" referred to in Daniel 9 are weeks of years—each "week" representing seven years. So "seven weeks and sixty-two weeks" would be 483 years, correlating (depending on how you count) with the period of time between the return of the exiles to Jerusalem and the death of Christ just outside of Jerusalem.

But what about the "seventy weeks" described in verse 24? Many conservative Bible interpreters believe that the seventieth "week" in this period—the final seven-year period in God's great redemption story—is yet to come and will be fulfilled at the end of the age, culminating with the return of Christ.

But again, we don't have to get hung up on the numbers. We don't have to be able to figure out the exact timetable. We just need to know that these numbers make perfect sense in the mind of God. He's the only One who needs to know them because He's the One in charge of them.

As you try to wrap your head around this complex passage, don't miss the main point of the angel's message, sent in response to Daniel's earnest prayer of confession and intercession: God has promised to put a stop to sin—to our sin, and to everything that sin has done to us—and to usher in a new world order where no sin of any sort exists. And He is doing it all through His Son, Jesus.

What greater hope could we possibly have?

The Bible is clear that there will be a day when Christ's work of redemption in our lives and the world is fully complete. On that day, the angel told Daniel, heaven's court will convene, the books will be opened (Dan. 7:10), and everyone whose name is found "written in the book will escape" (12:1).

The book of Revelation paints essentially the same picture, describing "the book of life of the Lamb who was slaughtered" (Rev. 13:8). All whose names are found inscribed in that book—those who have placed their faith in the sacrifice of Jesus for their sins—will be delivered from the eternal doom of the unrepentant unredeemed.

Daniel prayed for this day to come hundreds of years before Christ appeared on earth, before His ministry, His crucifixion, and His resurrection, and thousands of years (only God knows exactly how many) before the final events described in his visions. So don't ever think, when you're praying, that your prayers aren't traveling anywhere. God sent an angel to Daniel to report that God had heard Daniel's prayer and would do as Daniel asked. In fact, He was already doing it on a very specific timetable. And His plan for the redemption of His people is still unfurling today.

How long? He knows.

How will it end? *We* know.

Daniel's story, like every story, shows both our need for a

Savior and God's faithfulness in providing us salvation. And your story—my story, too—takes us right to His throne.

He wins. He saves. He rules.

Heaven rules.

And so we endure because He's already rescued us. We cling to faith because He's already promised us sight. We pray, "Your kingdom come. Your will be done on earth as it is in heaven" (Matt. 6:10) because we know what's being done in heaven: God's will, in God's time, in God's eternal victory. And because of Christ, by faith, we are living in that victory already, even as we wait and watch and pray here in this broken world.

TO THE END

Daniel was told, in reference to the hair-raising prophecies he'd seen, that

> "from the time the daily sacrifice is abolished and the abomination of desolation is set up, there will be 1,290 days. Happy is the one who waits for and reaches 1,335 days." (Dan. 12:11–12)

I can't do the math in my head that fast, but what in the world does this mean?

What it means to me is I can wait. You and I—we can wait. God is working, and so we can wait. God's timing is perfect, so we can and will wait. In fact, if we will wait on Him—even with all the things around us that we wish would hurry up—He has promised to make us happy and blessed. While we wait.

Psalm 112 promises us as much:

> Happy is the person who fears the LORD. . . .
> He will never be shaken.
> The righteous one will be remembered forever.
> He will not fear bad news;
> his heart is confident, trusting in the LORD.
> His heart is assured; he will not fear.
> In the end he will look in triumph on his foes.
> (vv. 1, 6–8)

I can live with that. I can wait, knowing that. Can't you? For this is life in the long view, as experienced in the short run.

My heart was first captivated by this "Heaven rules" theme some years ago, when I spent months journaling my way through the book of Daniel. When I came to the final chapters, I found myself wading through the lengthy, detailed apocalyptic visions, trying to understand what God intended for Daniel (and us) to take away from them. Here's how I finally summarized those chapters. It's what gives me the strength and hope I need to press on today and tomorrow and every day . . . until That Day.

> Powerful rulers
> Aggressive, arrogant
> Truth trampled
> Lies prevail

Saints persecuted
Sanctuary profaned

How long?!
God knows

Evildoers overthrown
Sanctuary restored
God wins
The end
Heaven rules
Forever.

CHAPTER NINE

Stars Shining Bright

Heaven rules,
and sprinkles our lives with wonder along the way.

—Dawn Wilson

IT'S CLEAR BY NOW, I feel sure, that I'm passionate about the subject of this book. "Heaven rules" has galvanized my thinking and worldview, my window on every day of my life, as significantly as "God is love" and "Jesus saves." I hope you're experiencing the same.

Once you begin looking for reminders that Heaven rules, you start to see it everywhere. You'll be reading along in your Bible, and there it is—another HR verse, another HR sighting. You'll hear a quote you like, maybe in a sermon or on a podcast, and then you'll notice—there it is again. Something is said that speaks to Heaven's rule, either the need for it or the reality of it.

Then a meteorologist on the TV news attributes that day's weather, either its beauty or its power, to the work of "Mother Nature." And you respond with *What? No!* because you're a "Heaven rules" thinker now.

You hear things differently. You see things differently.

More important, you respond to things differently.

As Daniel did.

He realized no earthly situation had *only* an earthly explanation, which meant that each earthly situation called for more than just a typical, earthly response. A human king, for example, could order Daniel's execution. But no human king could order Daniel's reaction or change his beliefs and priorities. Only God could do that.

Heaven ruled the world, so heaven ruled Daniel.

And so may heaven rule us—may the *God* of heaven rule us. This is what will fill us with courage and comfort in the midst of all of the chaos and battles we face here on earth.

Daniel 12 is a short chapter that brings Daniel's final vision to a close. Read this chapter, highlighting each reference to "the end." What precedes the end of time? What hope was Daniel given about the end? And what encouragement did he receive about how to live until then?

HR ACTION PLAN

"Heaven rules" is an active theology. It's not something tucked away in a folder in our mental or doctrinal filing system. It goes with us into our day. We pack it for the road. We keep it in our carry-on baggage. We pull it out and use it all the time.

We'd better. Because there's certainly a lot of action being taken against us.

Back in Daniel 11, where the coming movements and methods

of Antiochus Epiphanes are described (and by extension, the movements and methods of other antichrist rulers and the ultimate Antichrist yet to come), we read how this enemy would focus the brunt of his anger against the people of God (Dan. 11:28–35). "He will rage against the holy covenant and take action" (11:30).

"Take action." Can't you feel the force of that action being taken

> "Heaven rules" is an active theology. It goes with us into our day. We pack it for the road. We keep it in our carry-on baggage. We pull it out and use it all the time.

today against us and against our brothers and sisters around the world? It happens day after day—endless, wearying action against the truth and against those who love the truth.

So are we helpless to do anything about this? Do we just take it? Does a "Heaven rules" mindset lead us to a passive, inactive response in the face of evil?

Actually, there is something we can do. Something we *will* do if we know the King of heaven. Yes, the enemies of God will take action against the people of God. "But," the Scripture tells us, "the people who know their God will be strong and take action" too (11:32).

Not in the same way as our opponents. Not with rancor or ranting, not by hurling epithets on social media, not by returning evil for evil, not by looking to political parties or placing our hope in the latest promising candidate.

> For although we live in the flesh, we do not wage war
> according to the flesh, since the weapons of our warfare
> are not of the flesh, but are powerful through God for
> the demolition of strongholds. (2 Cor. 10:3–4)

So instead of taking action "according to the flesh," we take seriously the assurance of Scripture that "Heaven rules" and that in the end God wins. And then we let that perspective shape everything about how we think and respond and interact in this world.

What does that look like? Here are ten takeaways from the life of Daniel that will be evident in us if we truly believe that Heaven rules:

HR TAKEAWAY #1: **We resolve to live as holy people of a holy God rather than assimilating into the culture around us.**

Heaven's rule means God's truth is both constant and eternal. In contrast, public opinions and policies change with the times and may pressure us to shift our standards as well. But HR people stay tethered to God's Word as their guide for all of life.

Daniel, you recall, even as a teenager, resolved he would not defile himself with the requirements of the king's program in whatever way it deviated from what his conscience allowed. He and his friends were willing to swim upstream rather than go with the mainstream to gain the flattering acceptance of those around them. Devotion to the Most High was their main motivation. May that be so for us today.

HR TAKEAWAY #2: **We don't panic or despair when the enemies of God seem to be winning, when hard things happen, when our freedoms are threatened, or when comforts are removed from us.**

"Lord, our world is upside down!" Those words were said by my husband as we were praying just before bed one night not long ago. It's true. Our world is indeed upside down. Daniel's world was upside down too. And, though I'm loath to say it, our world will almost certainly be staying upside down until Jesus comes to turn it right side up again and to give us a whole "new earth" (Rev. 21:1).

Between now and then, evil will continue to run amok, troubles will overwhelm us, morals will rush downhill, age and sickness will deplete us. But heaven still rules, and we can live in that assurance. As a result we can walk with calm and contentment through circumstances that send other people into a tizzy.

I'm not saying our emotions will never flare. They will. They do. But keeping a "Heaven rules" perspective reminds us of what is true and ultimate, settles our anxious hearts, and protects us from becoming panicked by the convulsions of this present world.

HR TAKEAWAY #3: **We give up trying to control people and circumstances.**

People who aren't convinced that Heaven rules have a tendency to think God's job must be theirs. But what a burden playing God can become. And what a gift to know it's not required of us. The pressure to change people, the nagging for our voice to be heard, the manipulation for gaining time and advantage—they're gone. Consider their reign at an end. You and I can live without all of them, once we truly believe our God is ruling from heaven and is working everything toward His superior purposes. Instead of spinning our wheels to get others moving at our speed and in our direction, we can trust Him, stay in our place, and . . .

> ∧
> What a burden playing God can become. And what a gift to know it's not required of us.
> ∨

HR TAKEAWAY #4: **We pray.**

Of all the things to learn and apply from Daniel, this may be the most powerful—and the most needful. Daniel habitually "turned [his] attention to the Lord God to seek him by prayer" (Dan. 9:3). If we believe that Heaven rules, this will be our habit as well. If there is a God who rules, as Daniel believed and as we believe, why would we not look to Him for help and answers rather than to the government, the courts, elections, or anything or anyone else?

If you've been searching for encouragement and the impetus to take a deeper, more fervent dive into prayer, then a "Heaven rules" perspective might be just what you need. Looking at life through the HR lens makes doing almost anything other than prayer seem unproductive by comparison.

HR TAKEAWAY #5: **We live as people of hope rather than people of outrage.**

When people observe the church and Christians, I'm afraid that too often they see us either working really hard to gain society's acceptance and approval or else making a lot of angry, ugly noise in opposition to the world. But the HR principle guards us against either faulty extreme.

Do we abandon biblical truth for the sinking ship of cultural accommodation? Of course not. But must we express our frustrations by bludgeoning other people who, yes, are fallen and sinful (as are we, apart from Christ), but who also desperately need God's mercy? Not at all.

God's Word, despite the condition of our world, gives us hope that He is at work and that His way will prevail without our needing to thrash other sinners with the truth.

HR TAKEAWAY #6: **We serve God faithfully where He has placed us.**

In Daniel 8 we read about an intense vision that left Daniel "overcome and . . . sick for days" (v. 27). The verse goes on to tell us what he did next: "Then I got up and went about the king's business."

Did you catch that? Daniel went back to work—in Babylon, serving a pagan king. None of his bosses or the administrations he worked under shared his belief system. People around him overtly sought to undermine his influence. He possessed little

> We have been placed in our current situation by God, and we are to serve wherever He has put us—in our workplaces, schools, neighborhoods, and nations—while keeping our hearts firmly planted in heaven.

in the way of emotional or spiritual support from others. And yet he added value to every environment where he served. He showed respect to those in leadership, even when they were fickle and unreasonable in their expectations. God had put him there in Babylon, and that is where he represented the kingdom of his God.

Yes, he was burdened about the distressing events he'd learned would fall on the earth in years to come. And he was well aware that Babylon and all other earthly kingdoms yet to come would eventually crumble and come to nothing. In the meantime, however, he faithfully went about the work God had given him to do in the king's service—knowing that ultimately he was serving the King of heaven.

We live in a fallen world and work in human systems that are destined to fail. There are deeply disturbing things going on around us, and we may sometimes feel overwhelmed and sick about it all. Yet we have been placed in our current situation by God, and we are to serve wherever He has put us—in our workplaces, schools, neighborhoods, and nations—while keeping our hearts firmly planted in heaven and holding fast to the hope that the purposes and promises of God will be fulfilled.

Rather than decry our situation, let's just see what faithfulness and integrity look like inside it. That's an HR testimony.

HR TAKEAWAY #7: We resist pride and pursue humility.

Scratch beneath all the misperceptions of Heaven's rule—the reasons we fight it or struggle to believe it—and you'll find that pride is always high on the list of contributing factors. We depend on our pride to defend us, protect us, and keep others from taking advantage of us. But being set free from pride, as HR allows us to be, frees us from so much that works against us: relational barriers, vocational distress, offended nerves, pointless comparisons. Much of what made Daniel's life so effective and inspirational was his humility. When we right-size our view of God and our view of ourselves, life begins to look totally different.

HR TAKEAWAY #8: We remain steadfast and calm in a culture that is chaotic and out of control.

A level-headed, long-view sense of steadiness is one of the greatest blessings you can bring to your family, your church, your work environment, and anywhere else that can sometimes be characterized by hostility and conflict.

Why do people lose control? Why do we ourselves sometimes lose control? Because we're crying out for someone to *take* control, somebody to make everything right! And yet all our situations, even the most stressful and unsolvable ones, are *already* under Someone's control.

Most people don't operate from this paradigm, and so they scramble and fume and vent and quit. But your belief in Heaven's rule can make your calm voice the loudest one in the room.

HR TAKEAWAY #9: **We believe God can change the heart of the proudest, most ungodly leader.**

Remember King Nebuchadnezzar, who rescinded his rash decree? King Darius, who altered his religious perceptions? And don't forget King Cyrus, the Persian king who ruled Babylon near the end of Daniel's time there (Dan. 10:1), who reversed seventy years of established policy in Babylon by allowing the Judean exiles to go home (2 Chron. 36:22–23).

Leaders' hearts can be changed. God can change them. He may not do it in ways we expect or follow the timeline we were hoping for. But as HR believers, that's what we pray for. And meanwhile we exercise patience. We choose forgiveness. We keep setting the example, as Daniel did, of how real faith lives.

Whether the leaders in question are in your home, in your office, in your church, in your national capital, or at any level of influence over you, don't despair over their hardheartedness. God has them in His hand.

HR TAKEAWAY #10: **We see every crisis in our world and in our lives as an opportunity for the impotence of false gods to be exposed and for the greatness and power of the living God to be displayed.**

In other words, adversity and difficulty are not things to be avoided at all costs. Besides, they'll come seeking us anyway. (Our enemy is looking to "take action" against us, remember?) We couldn't avoid them even if we tried.

But not only should we live expecting challenges; we can live making the most of them. Our witness for Christ stands out the most vividly in times of crisis. Our greatest impact is felt in those moments when it's hardest to believe that "Heaven rules" and yet by faith we keep our hearts and minds steadily tethered to Christ. That's when we as "people who know [our] God" show Him strong by taking action.

It's all part of our HR action plan, which turns us from worriers into warriors; from hard-luck stories into long-suffering, overcoming survivors and victors; from complainers into compelling examples of God's reigning power and glory. Our lives testify to all who see us that they too can take His truth as living gospel.

INSIGHT AND INFLUENCE

As we see in Daniel, our *insight*—our HR insight—gives us *influence*.

> "The people who know their God will be strong and take action. Those who have insight among the people will give understanding to many." (Dan. 11:32–33)

The Hebrew verb translated "have insight" in this passage is *sakal*.[1] This important word is used nine times in the book of Daniel.[2] It can mean "to be wise," "to understand," to "have skill," or to "have insight" and is sometimes translated as an adjective like "wise" or a noun like "understanding." It refers to the wisdom, skill, and understanding that everyone wants but only God's people can have.

Sakal makes us different. It makes our faith unmistakable. And according to the words spoken to Daniel by the angel,

> "Those who have insight [*sakal*] will shine
> like the bright expanse of the heavens,
> and those who lead many to righteousness,
> like the stars forever and ever." (Dan. 12:3)

Paul would later say essentially the same thing, describing how the "children of God," as we live out our faith among "a crooked and perverted generation" are able to "shine like stars in the world, by holding firm to the word of life" (Phil. 2:15–16).

We're told in Proverbs 19 that "a prudent [*sakal*] wife is from the Lord" (v. 14). Her wisdom and insight make her a blessing to her husband and family. She shines as a light against the dark background of her times.

Daniel was a *sakal* man. Taken captive as a young teen by an idolatrous nation that hated Jews, he lived in a pagan world that loved darkness rather than light. Once in Babylon, he was placed by God in strategic positions of influence. He had access to the most powerful leaders in the world and was promoted to high-ranking positions. But he never let his success go to his head. He never allowed himself to get absorbed into the heady culture around him. He didn't grasp for self-advancement or seek to make a name for himself. His God-given wisdom, understanding, and skill, coupled with his humble, prayerful demeanor, made him a bright light that stood out as stars do on the darkest of nights. His life made a difference. *Sakal* men and women always do.

Some time ago, as I was first preparing to teach the book of Daniel through the "Heaven rules" lens, I learned that the husband of a friend of mine, a committed Christian, had been selected to be the president of one of the top universities in the United States—a Division 1 school with tens of thousands of students. This was a great honor. But from the news reports surrounding his appointment, it was clear that this man would have his work cut out for him. He would be facing a number of difficult issues for which he would need supernatural wisdom, grace, and protection.

I texted my friend, explained what I'd been studying, and told her it seemed to me that her husband was a modern-day Daniel. I attached a picture of Briton Rivière's famous painting titled *Daniel's Answer to the King.*[3] It shows the elderly Daniel standing erect and composed in the underground stone room where he'd spent the night. Half a dozen lions pace behind him—mouths closed, of course. Daniel gazes up toward the window where, presumably, Darius is standing after his (the king's!) restless night. The most striking aspect of the picture is the golden light that pours in from that window, shining on and around Daniel.

The old man's face almost seems to glow.

I wrote to my friend:

> I'm praying for you and [your husband] as you start
> into this new chapter. I'm sure there will be hard
> moments and rough patches, but heaven and the angels
> are standing watch and ready to rise up on your behalf
> anytime God says the word! [I had been living in Daniel
> 12 that week and had angels on my mind!]

After sharing with her the passage from Daniel 12:3 about those who have insight (*sakal*) shining like stars, I concluded: "What a gift you are to your husband—for such a time as this! And what a gift he will be to this institution and to those with whom he serves." *Sakal* people don't necessarily have easy lives, but they bring light and blessing to all around them.

Just as Daniel served a succession of kings in Babylon, this university president is serving the board and the leaders of a huge secular institution. But like Daniel, he knows that ultimately he is serving "the King." This *sakal* couple is living for eternity and for the kingdom of God that will never end. As a result, their lives are shining as bright lights, pointing many to Christ.

Even with enemy forces working against us, even with the steady rain of conflict coming down on our heads (the result of spiritual kingdoms in conflict), we are not paralyzed in the process. We are not rendered helpless. Instead we're enabled to live out the truth of our convictions, the insight our God has given us. Not only does He cover us with His comfort, not only does He empower us with His courage; by enlightening us with His wisdom, He makes us reflectors of His light in a dark world simply as we "take action" each day.

Nothing ugly. Nothing harsh and grating. Just a single-focused, *sakal*-inspired, HR mindset and lifestyle.

And I think I speak for you and me when I say I want in on that action.

I want my words, my example, my response to hardship and pressure—my whole life—to declare that the future is fully known to God and that all of it is under His control: my future, your future, your family's future, your spouse and children's future. Our world, our days, our health, our steps.

Everything is His, and He rules over all:

- over all powers, nations, governments, and kings
- over all of history—past, present, and future
- over dictators, despots, and dynasties
- over national elections and political parties
- over financial markets and world economies
- over geopolitical spheres and affairs
- over the world of science and nature
- over weather patterns and storms
- over changes in the climate
- over the planets in orbit
- over the seasons
- over the sun

And just as nothing escapes His rule and attention in the macro, He rules with equal care over everything that touches us in the micro:

- over hurts and wounds that no one else knows about
- over unfulfilled longings for a mate or a child
- over financial challenges and retirement plans
- over relational problems and prodigal children
- over inattentive or even unfaithful spouses
- over health issues and job concerns

This is what He has said He is doing. He is in control of all of these things and more. And so this is what I intend to do, and I invite you to come join me: to live in such active alignment with these truths from His Word that He can make our lives into stars shining bright, living examples that proclaim, "Heaven rules." For us and for them. For our good and for His glory.

GO ON YOUR WAY

Oh, how I've loved getting to know Daniel through this study. His heart. His faith. The courage and calm behind his principles. The life he lived both in public and in private. The things God did through him. The way God lit up Daniel's world around him, for all to see, through his simple trust and daring faithfulness.

Yet one of my favorite images of him comes in the final chapter of the book of Daniel. By then Daniel had seen and heard the last of the prophecies he recorded for us in Scripture.

He'd listened, he'd looked, he'd watched. He'd endured the pulse-pounding sight of beasts the size of sea monsters and even beheld the Ancient of Days, clothed in light and fire upon His throne. He'd fainted and swooned a few times during his visions. We'd have fainted a few times ourselves.

And can't you just hear the puzzlement in Daniel's voice when he looked up at the end of it all and said, "I heard but did not understand" (Dan. 12:8).

Daniel was brilliant. Daniel loved learning. He wanted to make sense of these difficult things that even a wise, insightful man like himself couldn't seem to grasp. He'd heard it. He'd seen it. He just didn't quite know what to make of all of it.

Tell me you don't know that expression on his face. Tell me you haven't felt the same sense of bewilderment. *What is God doing? What is He saying? Why is He allowing this? What does this mean?*

We hear it. We're just not sure we understand it. We do know that Heaven rules. We believe it. God's Word convinces us of it. We're not budging from that conviction. It's become how we think and live. But it takes place around circumstances in our lives that are so hard to process and live through. So on some mornings we still struggle to fathom how Heaven's rule and these situations can coexist.

But I am settled by the angel's reply to Daniel's request for understanding. It's enough of a nonanswer that you almost need to sit with it a minute before its impact washes over you. But when it does, you realize it's the perfect answer:

"Go on your way, Daniel." (Dan. 12:9)

"As for you, go on your way to the end." (12:13)

Daniel was an elderly man by now. But he was to keep on keeping on—not settle into a life of leisure, not assimilate into the godless culture around him, but go on living as a faithful servant of the Lord in a foreign land all the way "to the end" of his life. To trust that God was capably taking care of all that he couldn't understand.

What would happen at the end? "You will rest," God promised Daniel, "and then you will rise to receive your allotted inheritance at the end of the days" (12:13).

At the end of his earthly life, after he had served and labored faithfully, Daniel would enter into that *rest* for which he had labored. At the end of the age, he would *rise* and be resurrected. And then he would be *rewarded*.

Rest. Resurrection. Reward. That's what Daniel had to look forward to. And that is what you and I have to look forward to as well.

This is the word of God to all of His people: "As for you, go on your way." Don't worry about what everyone else is doing in these crazy times. Just keep serving, be faithful, and endure all the way "to the end," holding fast to the assurance that Heaven rules.

And this is His promise: "You will rest, and then you will rise to receive your allotted inheritance." Our reward is then, not now.

So keep going, and let Heaven keep ruling around you and through you. One of these days, as with Daniel, God will call you to "rest, and then you will rise." Resurrected out of this corruptible body, you will live eternally in His presence under His majestic and loving rule, with nothing to fight or interfere with it ever again.

- Your pressures and your problems will not have the final say.
- Those who mock God and reject His truth will not have the final say.
- Wicked rulers and cruel family members will not have the final say.
- Those who persecute God's people will not have the final say.
- Filthy demons of hell will not have the final say.
- Sickness and soreness will not have the final say.
- Sin and its side effects will not have the final say.
- Not even death itself will have the final say.

"Go on your way," Daniel.

Heaven is ruling.

Those Who Know Their God

"The people who know their God
will be strong and take action."

—*Daniel 11:32*

WE'VE MET QUITE A FEW significant characters in the book of Daniel.

A number of these were "somebodies" on the world stage: notably King Nebuchadnezzar of Babylon and his Babylonian and Medo-Persian successors, each surrounded by a constellation of nobles and counselors. By earth's reckoning these were powerful men, renowned and revered as leaders, warriors, monarchs, and influencers.

We've also been introduced to Daniel and three other Hebrew captives. By contrast to the kings they served, they were "lesser lights" in Babylon, even less luminous elsewhere in the known world. From earth's perspective their power, influence, and control were limited—rising or falling according to the whims of their superiors and peers. Much of the time they were forced to swim upstream against the cultural, political, and religious currents of their day.

We've discovered that behind these very human historical figures and events, unseen forces were at work—the so-called gods of Babylon (actually representing demonic activity[1]) and the God of Israel, the former contending against the latter in a cosmic struggle for control.

Right from the get-go, for instance, we saw "the house of [Nebuchadnezzar's] god" at war against "the house of [Daniel's] God" (Dan. 1:2). Ancient people believed that if a king conquered another nation's gods, he proved that his god was more powerful. Nebuchadnezzar was saying, in effect, "My god is better than your God!" Daring the God of Israel to vindicate Himself, to speak up for Himself.

Battle on.

What has become apparent is that all of these men, the godless and the godly, were bit players compared to the Main Character of this drama—as are all humans, no matter what their credentials and résumés may claim.

The kings who ruled through the course of Daniel's lifetime thought of themselves as a big deal, and they liked it that way. It mattered to them to be known.

But what mattered to Daniel and his friends was not being known, but knowing the one, true, and living God. And they wanted all those around, beneath, and above them to know their God too.

As I've lingered repeatedly in the book of Daniel over the past few years, one of the most striking things to me has been to see the centrality of Daniel's God throughout. Now, of course, we know that God is central in all of Scripture, from cover to cover. But this book (unlike, say, the nearby book of Esther, which ironically contains no direct references to God) contains nearly eighty references to God in its twelve chapters, including over two dozen different names, titles, and descriptions for God!

Try looking through the book of Daniel and highlighting every explicit reference to God. Make a list of what you find about who He is and what He does. You'll find this a deeply encouraging reminder that our God is bigger, greater, and more real than anything that may be pressing in your life or our world in this season. In the words of the psalmist: "Those who know your name trust in you" (Ps. 9:10).

Here's what I want you to see: Daniel knew his God.

That's what made him strong—able to withstand the powerful, anti-God forces of his day. That's what gave him courage to "take action" in the name of his God when kings and lawmakers were taking action *against* his God. That's what comforted him in the face of unwanted changes and unexpected losses. And that's what kept him calm despite the swirl of cultural chaos and upheaval all around him.

Knowing your God will do the same for you.

You see, just as the theme of the whole Bible, in one sense, is "Heaven rules," the whole purpose of our life, in another sense, is knowing the God of heaven—heeding what He's made known to us about Himself in Creation, in His Word, and through His Son; experiencing Him amid the problems and pressures of each day; and making Him known to others.

> /\
> The whole purpose of
> our life is knowing the
> God of heaven.
> \/

It's not just that Heaven rules, but that the God who rules from heaven is real. This God is powerful. He is near. He is kind. He is high and lifted up, and there is nothing unknown to Him. Yet He is knowable to us—yes, to *us*—and is eager to relate to us on a deeply personal level.

And in our look at Daniel's story, we have seen that who God is has everything to do with our story as His children: what we eat, how we do our work, how we respond to unexpected crises, how we live as children of God in a world that opposes Him, how we respond to unreasonable or ungodly supervisors, and how we respond to laws that require us to violate biblical convictions.

KNOWING GOD BY NAME

I don't have to tell you that our world is coming apart at the seams—or so it seems. Contention, anger, violence are at a fever pitch. We're dealing with overt, in-your-face rejection of God and His Word, and the conflict between good and evil is becoming more intense on every front.

That's why we need to know our God—this God who rules and reigns forever, over every king and kingdom, over every confusing circumstance, every painful trial, every false ideology, and every determined opponent.

And that's why it seems fitting to end this book by highlighting several of the names and descriptions of our God that are found in the book of Daniel. (I've included a complete list in the appendix.) You'll discover fresh springs of grace and peace as you ponder what these names reveal about His character and His ways.

God

By my count, this name (or variations of it) appears more than fifty times in the book of Daniel. It is the first name for God we encounter in Scripture: "In the beginning God created the heavens and the earth" (Gen. 1:1). The Hebrew *Elohim* or its shortened form, *El,* refer to "the supreme One, the mighty One." This is the God who gave Daniel favor with his pagan captors (Dan. 1:9) and an understanding of the times (1:17). It's the name Daniel used when he gave thanks in prayer (6:10), the "great and awe-inspiring God" who captured Daniel's worship (9:4), yet who tenderly loved and "treasured" Daniel (10:19), just as He loves and treasures us.

The Lord

In almost all our English translations of the Bible, this name for God is written like this: Lord—with capital "L" and "ord" in small caps. Our English rendering of the Hebrew consonants for this name would be *YHWH* (often written as *Yahweh*).

This is God's personal name, the one He revealed to Moses at the burning bush: "the Lord, the God of your ancestors, the God of Abraham, Isaac, and Jacob" (Ex. 3:16). This name speaks of His self-existence and His unchanging eternality. Daniel addressed Him in prayer as the "Lord my God" (Dan. 9:4)—the covenant-keeping "Lord our God" who "is righteous in all he has done" (9:14).

The Lord

The Hebrew name *Adonai* is also translated as "Lord," but without the capital letters—not as a way of diminishing it, but simply as a way of identifying it. This name of God is more akin to how we understand *lord* in common usage, as an owner or landlord. We are His servants, and He is above us, sovereign over us.

"He's got the whole world in His hands," in other words.

This is the "Lord" who "handed King Jehoiakim of Judah over" to Nebuchadnezzar (Dan. 1:2), and the "Lord" whom Daniel asked to "turn away" His wrath "from your city Jerusalem, your holy mountain" (9:16).

The Most High

This name, frequently featured in the book of Daniel, tells us that there are none higher, there are none equal, there are none who can compare with this God. He is bigger. He is greater. He is more powerful than any other god.

In that passage where Daniel interpreted the dream Nebuchadnezzar had seen about the great tree, the one that had been cut down and left as a stump, he announced it as being "the decree of the Most High" (Dan. 4:24). The king's insanity that followed would last until he acknowledged that "the Most High is ruler over human kingdoms, and he gives them to anyone he wants" (4:25). "Heaven rules," of course (4:26), is another way, among many ways, of putting it.

God of my ancestors

Some translations render this "God of my fathers." The point is that Daniel recognized he was part of a long line and legacy of faith. As he looked back, he rehearsed how God had been faithful to those who came before him, and he knew that same God would be faithful to him:

> I offer thanks and praise to you,
> God of my ancestors,
> because you have given me
> wisdom and power. (Dan. 2:23)

When we look back and see how God was faithful to Daniel and to those three other Hebrew young men, we are reminded that God will also be faithful to us, because He is the God of our ancestors too—perhaps not our physical forebears but, for sure, our spiritual ones. The God that was Daniel's God—the God of Abraham (and Sarah), Isaac (and Rebekah), Jacob (and Rachel and Leah), Joseph (and his brothers)—that same God is our God.

The God who holds your life-breath in His hand
and who controls the whole course of your life

That's a long "title" for God, but it's an amazing one. Job tells us,

> The life of every living thing is in his hand,
> as well as the breath of all humanity. (Job 12:10)

Breath—it's the most essential human need. You can't live without breath, and you can't breathe without God. We are utterly dependent on Him for everything about our lives. And this is true of every person on the planet, no matter how powerful or invincible they may think they are.

This is the way Daniel described God to Belshazzar on the very night that the Babylonian king was killed and his kingdom was given to Darius the Mede (Dan. 5:23). All because the king refused to glorify this God.

Him who lives eternally

This name is from the vision recorded in Daniel 12:7. It attests to the reality that there will never, ever be a time, in this age or in eternity, when God will not be God, when He will not be present, when He will not be in control, when He will not be sovereign over every detail of our lives.

If you want to have a "Heaven rules" mindset, devote yourself to the task and the joy of knowing God. As you meditate on the divine names and titles found in the book of Daniel and elsewhere in Scripture, on what they reveal about who He is and what He does, you will "be strong" and know how to "take action." You'll take courage and comfort as you get to know this God who is in control. May He be praised forever.

Names, Titles, and Descriptions of God in the Book of Daniel

THE NAMES BELOW are listed in the order of their first appearance in the book of Daniel. Different Bible translations render some of these slightly differently, but the essence is the same. In cases where a name has many references, I have listed representative verses.

Rather than just glancing at this list, I hope you'll take a deeper dive into these names, one at a time, over the course of the next days, weeks, or even months. Read the verses where each one appears. Look it up in a Bible dictionary or commentary or on a site like BlueLetterBible.org. Jot down what you learn about the meaning and significance of each name or description, along with any personal reflections on what it means for faithful believers living in a faithless world.

1. God (1:2, 9, 17; 2:20; 5:23, 26; 9:11, 18, 23; 10:19)

2. The Lord (1:2; 9:7, 16, 17, 19)

3. The God of the heavens/God in heaven (2:18, 19, 28)

4.   God of my ancestors (2:23)

5.   God in heaven (2:28)

6.   Your God (2:47)

7.   God of gods (2:47)

8.   Lord of kings (2:47)

9.   Revealer of mysteries (2:47)

10. The God we serve (3:17)

11. The Most High God (3:26; 4:2; 5:18, 21)

12. The Most High (4:17, 24, 25, 32, 34; 7:18, 22, 25, 27)

13. The God of Shadrach, Meshach, and Abednego (3:28)

14. Ruler over human kingdoms (4:17)

15. The King of the heavens (4:37)

16. The God who holds your life-breath in His hand and who controls the whole course of your life (5:23)

17. His God (6:5, 10)

18. Your God, whom you continually serve (6:16)

19. The living God (6:20, 26)

20. My God (6:22)

21. The God of Daniel (6:26)

22. The Ancient of Days (7:9, 13, 22)

23. The Lᴏʀᴅ (9:2, 8, 14)

24. The Lord God (9:3)

25. The Lᴏʀᴅ my God (9:4, 20)

26. The Lord our God (9:9)

27. The Lᴏʀᴅ our God (9:10, 13)

28. Our God (9:17)

29. Him who lives eternally (12:7)

With Gratitude

HOW THANKFUL I AM for "my coworkers in Christ Jesus" (Rom. 16:3) whose assistance on this book has been indispensable and deeply encouraging.

For starters, I so appreciate two friends whose collaboration on numerous books over the years means more than I can express:

- *Lawrence Kimbrough* starts with transcripts of my teaching and masterfully organizes and shapes them into an initial manuscript—which in this case proved to be more challenging than either of us anticipated. He is a true artist and a gifted communicator.

- *Anne Christian Buchanan* is a consummate editor with an extraordinary eye and care for details. She patiently, painstakingly worked with me through several rounds of edits to clarify and hone this message.

In addition, I am indebted to:

- The Moody Publishers team—especially *Judy Dunagan, Ashley Torres, Erik Peterson,* and *Connor Sterchi*—for their heart for this project from the outset and for being true partners in ministry.

- *Dr. Chris Cowan* for providing biblical and theological review and helpful input on parts of the manuscript where

I had questions or wanted to double-check interpretive issues. Having this trusted lifeline has been a great gift.

- The Revive Our Hearts team, who serve with and support me every day in countless ways. *Janine Nelson*, our Senior Director of Advancement, is a cherished fellow servant who cares a lot about this message and about how to multiply its reach and impact.

- *Erik Wolgemuth*, my kind, capable agent, who somehow manages to keep track of the details for each book project I've got in the pipeline (including, but not limited to: "Can you remind me how many words this contract calls for?" . . . "When is that manuscript due?") and who finds joy in helping his clients publish Christ-exalting content.

- *Robert Wolgemuth*—aka my DH (my dear husband, who, by the way, connected me to Lawrence Kimbrough and Anne Buchanan years ago)—for his relentless love, shepherd's heart, and wise counsel, and for always being willing to engage when I say for the umpteenth time, "Which phrase do you think sounds better?" or "Can you help me think of a verb that means . . . ?" Both of us have written a new book this year. What a sweet season it has been as we worked side by side, assembling words that we pray will minister grace to you, the reader.

Recommended Resources

Numerous resources have been valuable to me in sorting through the historical details (who lived and ruled when and where) as well as various interpretive matters (mostly related to visions and prophecies) in the book of Daniel. I have not included citations for facts that are widely known and agreed upon or for interpretations gleaned from multiple commentaries where there is general consensus among conservative interpreters.

The following websites offer many Greek and Hebrew language tools as well as study Bibles, concordances, dictionaries, and commentaries that I often refer to for help in understanding particular passages:

- BibleGateway.com
- BibleHub.com
- BibleStudyTools.com
- BlueLetterBible.org
- EnduringWord.com
- PreceptAustin.org

As helpful as these tools can be, of course, there's no substitute for careful, repeated, prayerful reading and meditation on the Scripture itself.

Notes

Preface: Samuel's Story

1. Nancy DeMoss Wolgemuth, "When You Need Courage (Daniel 1)," *Heaven Rules: Seeing God's Sovereignty in the Book of Daniel* podcast series, Revive Our Hearts, September 29, 2021, www.reviveourhearts.com/podcast/ revive-our-hearts/when-you-need-courage-daniel-1. This transcription of the podcast episode has been lightly edited for flow.

Chapter One: A Single Lens

Epigraph: Margaret Clarkson, *Grace Grows Best in Winter* (Grand Rapids: Eerdmans, 1984), 40–41, accessed January 27, 2022, https://gracequotes .org/topic/god-sovereignty.

1. Nancy DeMoss Wolgemuth and Robert Wolgemuth, *You Can Trust God to Write Your Story: Embracing the Mysteries of Providence* (Chicago: Moody Publishers, 2019), 60–61.

2. Ibid.

Chapter Two: The Story behind the Story

Epigraph: John Piper, "God Is Always Doing 10,000 Things in Your Life," Desiring God, January 1, 2013, www.desiringgod.org/articles/ god-is-always-doing-10000-things-in-your-life.

1. My telling of this story is based on information from the following three sources: John McNeill, "Lessons from Korean Mission in the Former Soviet Region," *International Bulletin of Mission Research* 36, no. 2 (April 2012), 78–82, www.internationalbulletin.org/issues/2012-02/2012-02- 078-mcneill.html; James Won, "How Stalin's Paranoia Led to a Whole Ethnic Group Being Forcibly Relocated to a Foreign Land," https://history ofyesterday.com/how-stalins-paranoia-led-to-a-whole-ethnic-group-being- forcibly-relocated-to-a-foreign-land-2ab31fb4f7a8; Jae Kyeong Lee, "South Korea's Great Missionary Movement—God's Sovereignty, Our Obedience," IMB, February 9, 2018, www.imb.org/2018/02/09/south-korea-mission- movement.

2. History.com editors, "Perestroika," History.com, updated November 14, 2019, www.history.com/topics/cold-war/perestroika-and-glasnost.

3. King Jehoiakim was captured at this time and taken as a prisoner to Babylon along with a number of his subjects, including Daniel and his

three friends. Nebuchadnezzar later reinstated Jehoiakim on his throne as a vassal king. See "Daniel 1 Commentary," Precept Austin, under the heading "Three Invasions of Judah by Babylon," updated May 19, 2020, www .preceptaustin.org/daniel_1_commentary.

4. Interpreters debate exactly *how* the food and wine would defile Daniel. Although many have assumed that the food wasn't kosher (i.e., in accordance with the Mosaic law), there were no Mosaic restrictions on drinking wine. According to Daniel 10:3, he only refused royal food temporarily, so it doesn't seem to be a kosher issue. Some commentators suggest that Daniel and his friends were seeking not to be dependent on the king. By not eating "the *king's* food" (1:8, 13, 15), they were expressing dependence on and devotion to the Lord for their sustenance and success.

5. For more about the names of God in Daniel, see the epilogue and appendix of this book.

Chapter Three: No Need to Panic

Epigraph: *Free Grace and Dying Love: Morning Devotions by Susannah Spurgeon*, previously published as *A Carillon of Bells* (Edinburgh, Scotland, UK: Banner of Truth, 2006), 31.

1. The information on Louis XIV in this and the next two paragraphs has been gleaned from Will Durant and Ariel Durant, *The Age of Louis XIV*, The Story of Civilization, vol. 8 (New York: Simon and Schuster, 1963), 3–18.

2. Durant and Durant, *Age of Louis XIV*, 3, 685.

3. Matthew Henry, *Matthew Henry's Commentary on the Whole Bible*, vol. 4 (Isaiah to Malachi) (1896; repr., Old Tappan, NJ: Revell, 1985), 1187.

4. Nancy DeMoss Wolgemuth, "He Cares," *Coronavirus, Cancer, and Christ* podcast series, Revive Our Hearts, December 29, 2020, www.reviveourhearts .com/podcast/revive-our-hearts/he-cares.

5. Mercifully, the Lord spared my mother's life and eventually restored her to health.

Chapter Four: Can I Get a Witness?

Epigraph: Joni Eareckson Tada, "Paralysis Was His Good Plan: How Predestination Changed My Suffering," Desiring God, October 12, 2020, www.desiringgod.org/articles/paralysis-was-his-good-plan.

1. This explanation is widely stated in commentaries. See, for example, David Guzik, "Daniel 3—Saved in the Fiery Furnace," Enduring Word, accessed February 10, 2022, https://enduringword.com/bible-commentary/daniel-3.

2. According to Open Doors, an organization that publishes the World Watch List, an annual ranking of the fifty most dangerous countries for Christians, "In just the last year [2021], there have been . . . over 340 million Christians living in places where they experience high levels of persecution and discrimination." See "Christian Persecution," Open Doors (website), accessed January 27, 2022, www.opendoorsusa.org/christian-persecution.

3. "Jason Crabb—'There's Something about That Name,'" Grand Old Opry, performance recorded live December 18, 2021, YouTube video, 5:29, accessed February 10, 2022, www.youtube.com/watch?v=TQTXGiS5yno.

4. Jill Lyman, "Bremen Man Loses Home to Tornado, Stops to Play Piano in Praise," 14 News, December 13, 2021, https://www.14news.com/2021/12/13/bremen-man-loses-home-tornado-stops-play-piano-praise/.

5. Jill Lyman, "From Destroyed Home to Grand Ole Opry Stage, Bremen Man Continues Song of Praise," 14 News, December 18, 2021, https://www.14news.com/2021/12/18/destroyed-home-grand-ole-opry-stage-bremen-man-continues-song-praise/.

Chapter Five: Humbled

Epigraph: C. S. Lewis, *Mere Christianity*, rev. and enlarged ed. (New York: HarperOne, 2015), 227.

Chapter Six: Look Up!

Epigraph: David Jeremiah with C. C. Carlson, *The Handwriting on the Wall: Secrets from the Prophecies of Daniel* (Nashville: W Publishing, 2019), 174.

1. This story was first told by British evangelist Charles Inglis (1848–1936), who got it directly from the ship's captain. See Charles Inglis, "Mr Müller and the Fog," Müllers.org, accessed February 10, 2022, www.mullers.org/find-out-more-1875.

Chapter Seven: Battle Cry

Epigraph: Bobby Scott, "Suffering Taught Me the Sovereignty of God," Desiring God, November 22, 2021, www.desiringgod.org/articles/suffering-taught-me-the-sovereignty-of-god.

1. Revive Our Hearts has produced a moving video of Colleen's story: Revive Our Hearts, "She Laughs at the Time to Come | Colleen's Story," video, Revive Our Hearts (website), accessed February 10, 2022, www.reviveour hearts.com/videos/she-laughs-at-the-time-to-come-colleens-story.

2. The actual word *antichrist* (Greek *antikhristos*) appears in the Bible in the epistles of 1 and 2 John, which speak of both this ultimate "Antichrist" as well as "many antichrists" throughout history who oppose Christ through false teaching and persecution of the saints. Sometimes the term is also applied to false messiahs and vicious rulers described in biblical prophecies.

3. The quotes from Mark and Michelle in this section are based on an update they gave to their local church family. You can view their testimony at Brandywine Grace Church Media, "Testimony on Self-Reliance from Mark and Michelle Leach," from the May 2, 2021, service at Brandywine Grace Church, Downingtown, PA, YouTube video, 14:45, accessed February 10, 2022, www.youtube.com/watch?v=Rf-vTj64VkM.

4. This passage is a reminder that we are to be, as Paul says, praying "at all times in the Spirit with every prayer and request" (Eph. 6:18) as a key aspect of spiritual warfare.

Chapter Eight: The Long View

Epigraph: Randy Alcorn, *Money, Possessions, and Eternity,* rev. ed. (Carol Stream, IL: Tyndale House, 2021), 38.

1. On Demand Entertainment, "Gal Gadot Leads a Star-Studded Cover of John Lennon's 'Imagine,'" YouTube video, 3:09, accessed February 10, 2022, www.youtube.com/watch?v=0fDIZj9BX9U.

2. "Heidelberg Catechism," translation approved by Synod 1975 of the Christian Reformed Church, Christian Reformed Church (website), accessed February 10, 2022, www.crcna.org/welcome/beliefs/confessions/ heidelberg-catechism.

3. If you think you've read this phrase before, it's because you have, just a few pages back. This phrase is repeated verbatim both in Daniel 11:35 and Daniel 12:10. How kind is it of God to remind Daniel—and us—not once, but twice, that our tribulations are purposeful and will result in our greater sanctification.

4. This wonderful spiritual seems to have been collected by John Wesley Work II, known as the first African American compiler of folk songs and spirituals. The first known publication was in *Folk Songs of the American Negro,* published in 1907 under the name of Work's brother, Frederick

Jerome Work. It was popularized in an arrangement by William L. Dawson in the 1930s and has been sung by many well-known artists, including Mahalia Jackson. See Azizi Powell, "Early Published Versions of the African American Spiritual 'Soon I Will Be Done (with the Trouble of the World)," *pancocojams* (blog), September 29, 2019, https://pancocojams .blogspot.com/2019/09/early-published-versions-of-african.html.

Chapter Nine: Stars Shining Bright

Epigraph: My dear friend Dawn Wilson has served as a researcher with Revive Our Hearts for many years. As I am writing this book, she is undergoing chemotherapy for a recurrence of multiple myeloma. This is how she signed an email to me recently.

1. "Lexicon: Strong's H7919 *śākal*," Blue Letter Bible, accessed February 15, 2022, www.blueletterbible.org/lexicon/h7919/kjv/wlc/0-1.

2. Daniel 1:4, 17; 9:13, 22, 25; 11:33, 35; 12:3, 10.

3. Briton Rivière was a British artist with Huguenot roots who lived from 1840–1920. *Daniel's Answer to the King* was painted in 1890. You can see an image of it at https://en.wikipedia.org/wiki/Briton_Rivi%C3%A8re#/ media/File:Briton_Riviere_-_Daniel's_Answer_to_the_King_ (Manchester_Art_Gallery).jpg.

Epilogue: Those Who Know Their God

1. See Deuteronomy 32:17, Psalm 106:37, and 1 Corinthians 10:20.

The Most High God
is ruler over human kingdoms
and sets anyone he wants over them.

He is the living God,
and he endures forever;
his kingdom will never be destroyed,
and his dominion has no end.

Heaven rules.

—DANIEL 5:21; 6:26; 4:26

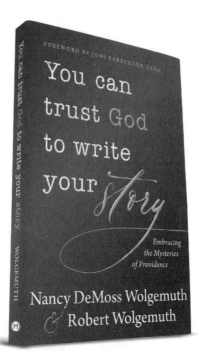